MOUNTA

WEST & SOUTH YORKSHIRE

HILLSIDE GUIDES - ACROSS THE NORTH

Long Distance Walks
- **THE COAST TO COAST WALK**
- **DALES WAY COMPANION**
- **THE WESTMORLAND WAY**
- **NORTH BOWLAND TRAVERSE**
- **FURNESS WAY**
- **CLEVELAND WAY COMPANION**
- **THE CUMBERLAND WAY**
- **LADY ANNE'S WAY**

Circular Walks - Lancashire
- **BOWLAND**
- **PENDLE & THE RIBBLE**

Circular Walks - Yorkshire Dales
- **HOWGILL FELLS**
- **THREE PEAKS**
- **MALHAMDALE**
- **WHARFEDALE**
- **NIDDERDALE**
- **WENSLEYDALE**
- **SWALEDALE**

Circular Walks - North York Moors
- **BOOK ONE - WESTERN MOORS**
- **BOOK TWO - SOUTHERN MOORS**
- **BOOK THREE - NORTHERN MOORS**

Circular Walks - South Pennines
- **BRONTE COUNTRY**
- **CALDERDALE**
- **ILKLEY MOOR**

Circular Walks - North Pennines
- **TEESDALE**
- **EDEN VALLEY**

Hillwalking - Lake District
- **OVER LAKELAND MOUNTAINS**
- **OVER LAKELAND FELLS**

Yorkshire Pub Walks
- **HARROGATE/WHARFE VALLEY**
- **HAWORTH/AIRE VALLEY**

Large format colour hardback
FREEDOM OF THE DALES

BIKING COUNTRY
- **YORKSHIRE DALES CYCLE WAY**
- **WEST YORKSHIRE CYCLE WAY**
- **MOUNTAIN BIKING - WEST & SOUTH YORKSHIRE**
- **AIRE VALLEY BIKING GUIDE**
- **CALDERDALE BIKING GUIDE**

- **WALKING COUNTRY TRIVIA QUIZ**
Over 1000 questions on the great outdoors

Send a S.A.E. for a detailed catalogue and pricelist

MOUNTAIN BIKING

WEST & SOUTH YORKSHIRE

Richard Peace

Photographs by

Paul Hannon & Richard Peace

HILLSIDE

HILLSIDE
PUBLICATIONS
11 Nessfield Grove
Keighley
West Yorkshire
BD22 6NU

First published 1996

© Richard Peace 1996
Illustrations © Paul Hannon/Richard Peace 1996

ISBN 1 870141 40 7

Whilst the author has cycled and researched all the routes for the purposes of this guide, no responsibility can be accepted for any unforeseen circumstances encountered while following them. The publisher would, however, greatly appreciate any information regarding material changes, and any problems encountered.

Cover illustration: Holden Gill, under Ilkley Moor
Back cover: Ascending to Midhope Moors;
White Wells, Ilkley; Ovenden Moor
(Paul Hannon/Big Country Picture Library)

Photo credits
Richard Peace: pages 28,35,61,65,79,91
Paul Hannon: pages 1,6,13,17,18,21,31,49,53,71,87

Printed in Great Britain by
Carnmor Print and Design
95-97 London Road
Preston
Lancashire
PR1 4BA

CONTENTS

ALSO BY RICHARD PEACE

- YORKSHIRE DALES CYCLE WAY
- WEST YORKSHIRE CYCLE WAY
- THE MACLEHOSE TRAIL (HONG KONG)

INTRODUCTION

The topography of West and South Yorkshire shows three distinct bands; the Pennines in the west which rise to over 500m (about 1600 feet) in places, and slope eastwards into the industrial and urban areas. This gradually turns into a flat plain in the east which ultimately stretches to the North Sea, broken only briefly in places by the Wolds. Thus the area offers a complete range of challenges to suit most mountain bikers, whether you're looking for steep climbs or you just want to enjoy a few miles on the flat as a beginner or with your family.

The routes cover the whole range of this varied scenery. For example the Grade 1 run from Tockwith is ideal for those just beginning to experiment with mountain biking or for those more experienced riders who want an easy relaxing ride. At the opposite end of the spectrum difficult Grade 3 climbs like that at Luddenden are only for fit cyclists with some experience who want a few testing climbs.

The routes chosen are not limited rigidly by the official boundaries of West and South Yorkshire but aim to give people living in the main industrial areas of the counties access to nearby interesting and legal routes and thus may 'slip over' into adjoining counties.

Approaching Ogden from Thornton Moor (Route 1)

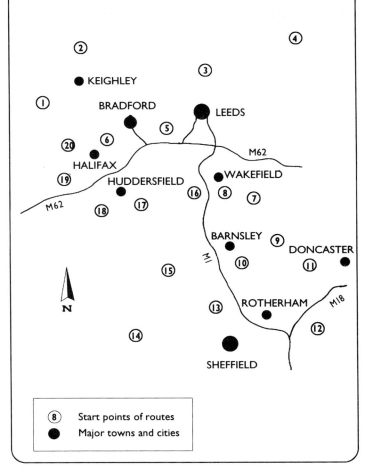

MOUNTAIN BIKING
WEST & SOUTH YORKSHIRE

④

②

● KEIGHLEY

③

①

BRADFORD

LEEDS

⑤

⑳ ⑥

M62

HALIFAX

⑲

WAKEFIELD

HUDDERSFIELD

⑯

⑧

⑱ ⑰

⑦

M62

BARNSLEY

⑨

DONCASTER

⑩

⑪

⑮

ROTHERHAM

M18

⑬

⑫

N

⑭

SHEFFIELD

| ⑧ | Start points of routes |
| ● | Major towns and cities |

EQUIPMENT

Clearly the most important piece of equipment is a bike that you can ride comfortably and safely. All the routes in this guide are really only suitable for mountain bikes, or at the very least the less common hybrid 'all terrain' bikes. You should know how to do basic maintenance and carry the following basic tools suitable for the jobs described. Because of the rougher conditions of mountain biking compared to going on the roads more maintenance is bound to be required:

- *Puncture repair kit, spare inner tubes, air pump* - for burst inner tubes
- *Tyre levers* - for burst inner tubes
- *Range of spanners* - changing of wheels if not quick release; other common adjustments e.g. if pedal becomes loose
- *Small screwdriver* - adjusting gear mechanisms
- *Adjustable spanner* - will fit a number of nuts on the bike if they work loose.
- *Allen keys* - to fit various adjustments: handlebar stem, seat post etc.
- *Chainsplitter* - this tool not only takes chains apart but you may be able to rejoin your chain if it breaks whilst riding.

Keep moving parts, especially the chain, well lubricated. For a complete guide to maintenance see *The Bike Book* (Haynes).

A helmet should always be worn and I found the most other useful clothes items to be:-
- Padded shorts or three-quarter length bottoms depending on the weather.
- Durable footwear with a chunky sole to grip the pedal. Some pedal systems have clips or the facility to 'screw' the underneath of a sole to the pedal which can be useful to keep your feet on the pedals over rough ground. Practice disengaging your feet quickly from the system so you can use it safely.
- Good waterproof, breathable tops and bottoms.
- 'Fingerless' cycling gloves.

You heat up quickly on a bike so you should have the capability to take off and add a couple of layers of clothing and keep dry spares in bike bags or a small backpack. Too much weight or too large a backpack will destabilise you.

RIDING TECHNIQUE

If you are a beginner the first thing you may notice is that riding off road up any kind of gradient is more difficult than road riding, because of the greater friction between tyres and surface. This effect varies according to the nature of the surface. Don't worry; take it easy and enjoy the scenery. For me the great joy of off road cycling is being able to go places and see things road cycling doesn't allow you to do.

Steep downhill sections require very close brake control. If you let them off for more than a second or two you can be seriously out of control. Don't try to force the bike where you think it ought to go; it will often run its own course if you concentrate on avoiding major obstacles. Relax your upper body and guide the bike; if you keep a very tight grip, hitting a small obstacle such as a stone is more likely to throw you off course.

On very steep uphill sections you may be able to cut across the track or road, if it is wide enough, in a zigzag pattern. You can start to do this if you think you will have to stop pedaling if you are heading straight up the hill. It effectively lessens your gradient and means you can take the climb in a more leisurely way. If you are on a road section watch out for traffic from behind.

Please keep to the tracks and ride under control and at sensible speed downhill. Mountain biking is rapidly gaining a bad name with other countryside users because of a few irresponsible riders. There have even been calls from certain quarters for legislation to ban mountain biking. Follow the code as set out overleaf.

ACCESS BY RAIL

There are various rules regarding the carrying of cycles on trains, depending on route, time and type of train! It would be a good idea therefore to get hold of the British Rail booklet *Cycling by Train*. It is available at most stations free of charge, and covers Reional Railways. It is likely the current situation will continue, with longer distance trips requiring a reservation and a £3 fee, and shorter routes within regional transport executive areas being generally free and on a 'first come, first served' basis, subject to peak hour restrictions. Because of the numerous rules and frequent changes, the best way is to ring the particular station you wish to use, or the nearest main station.

THE MOUNTAIN BIKE CODE OF CONDUCT
(with the author's additions in *italics*)

RIGHTS OF WAY

• *Bridleways* - open to cyclists but you must give way to walkers and horse riders. *Legally they should be signposted at junctions with public roads but this isn't always the case. Also note horses, especially young, nervous ones can be very scared of bikes. When they are coming in the opposite direction it is best to stop. When you approach from behind give a gentle 'excuse me' if you think the riders haven't heard you. If you scare a horse it can bolt causing injury to the rider or those nearby.*

• *Byways* - usually unsurfaced tracks open to cyclists. As well as walkers and cyclists you may meet occasional vehicles which also have a right of access.

• *Public footpaths* - no right to cycle exists. *There are very occasional sections in the routes where you have to use footpaths, and they are indicated in the directions. Please dismount and push your bike.*

Look out for posts from the highway or waymarking arrows (blue for bridleways, red for byways and yellow for footpaths).
NB The above rights do not apply in Scotland.

OTHER ACCESS

• *Open land* - on most upland, moorland and farmland cyclists normally have no right of access without the express permission of the landowner.

• *Towpaths* - a British Waterways cycling permit is required for cyclists wishing to use their canal towpaths.

• *Pavements* - cycling is not permitted on pavements

• *Designated cycle paths* - look out for designated cycle paths or bicycle routes which may be found in urban areas, on forestry commission land, disused railway lines or other open spaces.

OTHER INFORMATION

• Cyclists must adhere to the Highway Code. A detailed map is recommended for more adventurous trips.

THE COUNTRY CODE

- Enjoy the countryside and respect its life and work
- Guard against all risk of fire
- Fasten all gates
- Keep dogs under close control
- Keep to rights of way across farmland
- Use gates and stiles to cross fences, hedges and walls
- Leave livestock, crops and machinery alone.
- Take your litter home
- Help to keep all water clean
- Protect wildlife, plants and trees
- Take special care of country roads
- Make no unnecessary noise

SAFETY

- Ensure that your bike is safe to ride and prepared for all emergencies
- You are required by law to display working lights after dark (front and rear)
- Always carry some form of identification
- Always tell someone where you are going
- Learn to apply the basic principles of first aid
- Reflective materials on your clothes or bike can save your life (*obviously this applies doubly to road sections*)
- For safety on mountains refer to *Safety on Mountains,* a British Mountaineering Council publication (*this applies to some of the higher Pennine routes*)
- Ride under control when going downhill, since this is often when serious accidents occur
- If you intend to ride fast off road it is advisable to wear a helmet. (*I recommend it on all routes at all times*)
- Particular care should be taken on unstable or wet surfaces

RIGHTS OF WAY

Although the legal position is set out in the code of conduct above, the situation on the ground may not be that simple. There are many minor roads shown on maps but their status is not clear from the map alone and may need further research. Bridleways may be shown on a map but may not exist when you look for them or may be obstructed when you try to ride along them. Similarly many rights of way that exist for bikes may not be shown on the map.

These problems are solved by this guide; all routes were fully legal at the time of going to press and their legality has been researched extensively by the author. However it is still strongly recommended to take the appropriate map and a compass if you do happen to become lost. Pathfinder and Outdoor Leisure maps are most detailed, showing features such as individual fields. My own directions and maps will complement these maps, although bear in mind I occasionally point out bridleways that may not be marked as such on the maps.

Please stick to the tracks indicated. In particular mountain bikers going down footpaths and private roads in some areas have caused a severe backlash against the sport.

ABBREVIATIONS & SYMBOLS

Route descriptions
R - turn or bear right   **L** - turn or bear left
O - bridleway
¶ - signpost (usually a green roadside public bridleway sign)

Sketch maps
S - starting point of route
••• - route (arrows indicate direction)   **⌐** - roads
➤•➤ - route on roads   **-⌐⌐-** - other relevant tracks
⊕ - towns/villages   **⌐⌐⌐** rivers   **✕✕✕** - railways

Cross section diagrams
! - lung busting ascent
!! - as above, but take extra oxygen!
☠ - steep/tricky descent: hands on brakes and close control
☠☠ - extremely steep descent, in places: be very wary and ensure you can stop quickly if necessary.

Harewood House (Route 3)

SOME USEFUL ADDRESSES

Sustrans
35 King Street, Bristol BS1 4DZ
Tel. 01272-268893
(a charity that actually constructs off-road cycle routes)

Cyclists' Touring Club
Cotterell House, 69 Meadrow, Godalming, Surrey GU7 3HS
Tel. 01483-417217

British Cycling Federation
Stuart Street, Manchester M11 4DQ
Tel. 0161-2232244

South Pennines Packhorse Trails Trust
The Barn, Mankinholes, Todmorden OL14 6HR
Tel. 01706-815598
(does excellent work establishing and looking after bridleways)

1

OXENHOPE MOORS

START *Oxenhope*   *Grid ref. 032353*

DISTANCE COVERED   *18km/11 miles*
On road *8km/5 miles*   **Off road** *10km/6 miles*

TIME ALLOWED *3 hours*   **GRADIENT DIFFICULTY** *3*

ACCESS *Start from the railway station.* **Car** *roadside parking nearby: station car park is for railway users.* **Train** *Served by Worth Valley Railway from Keighley BR station.*

ORDNANCE SURVEY MAPS
1:50,000 - Landranger 104, Leeds, Bradford & Harrogate
1:25,000 - Outdoor Leisure 21, South Pennines

SUGGESTED BREAK   *By Ogden Reservoir at the midway point*

SUMMARY
A strenuous, high level circuit of the valley enclosing Haworth and Oxenhope. Steep early climbing is followed by a good mix of moorland tracks and old lanes linked by quiet roads.

S From the station entrance climb **L** up the steep Harry Lane to join the A6033 Hebden Road. Go **L** a couple of minutes to a sharp bend, then turn **R** up a track (¶ **O**) immediately after the house. This climbs steeply to end at a farm. A green way takes over, swinging right on the level, to be quickly replaced by another drive that climbs up onto Black Moor Road. Cross straight over and along an enclosed track, Cuckoo Park Lane (¶ *Senior Way*).

This emerges onto Black Moor, and a super run through the heather. There are good views over Cullingworth and the Aire Valley to a Rombalds Moor skyline. Above your impending route are the flapping sails of Ovenden Moor windfarm. This same track runs on through an old wall and along to a gate onto Trough Lane. Turn **R** to the Dog & Gun pub. Cross the B6141 and up Sawood Lane (**¶** *no through road*). A steep pull leads past the dwellings at Sawood, becoming a rough track to join a Water Authority road. There are now sweeping views over Leeming and its reservoir to Oxenhope, backed by Haworth's moors. Go **R** on this road, straight along the track as the road turns left to Thornton Moor Reservoir. Just beyond a **¶** *Bronte Way* the track turns **L** and forks.

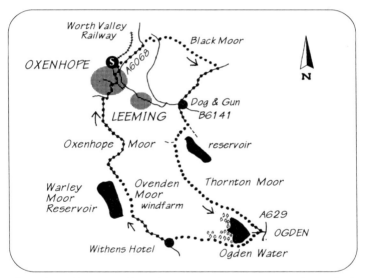

The **L** branch passes through a gate to commence a short climb between old walls. Partly sunken, a section here is likely to reduce most riders to a short walk until it eases out. The crest is quickly gained, a fence left behind, and the wind turbines flapping happily. A track runs on through the heather, slowly dropping towards the head of Ogden Clough. A wall is reached and followed for a while. At a fork remain with the wall, and the track soon becomes enclosed and part sunken between old walls again. As Back Lane it becomes firmer as it runs on and down to the Ogden Water road. Don't advance to the main Keighley-Halifax road just ahead (other than for refreshments at the tearooms) but turn **R** to the car park.

From the car park descend the road **L** past the information kiosk and across the dam. In this early section be prepared for many pedestrians, including young children, on sunny weekends. A broad track climbs away between a golf course on the left and a plantation on the right; the Withens Hotel waits patiently on the skyline. Though a lengthy pull to begin with, it is fairly easy and gets the final major climb over with quickly.

At the top the track levels out to reach the pub. Increasingly featuring in the scene are the wind turbines of Ovenden Moor. After possible refreshment at the highest pub in West Yorkshire, turn **R** along the road. The windfarm is soon passed and the road runs on above Warley Moor Reservoir. Stoodley Pike is prominent over to the left amidst the Calderdale moors. This is a long, easy section at very high altitude. Other than on Sundays this road is virtually empty, being little more than a rough track for quite a spell. At the end it begins a long descent towards Oxenhope as Nab Water Lane. The Haworth and Worth Valley area is outspread ahead.

The latter stage is particularly steep, so caution is needed. Brake in good time at the bottom as you are joining the A6033 Hebden Bridge road. Turn **R** down through a hairpin bend and into the top end of

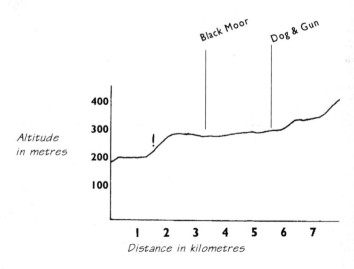

16

The Bay Horse, Oxenhope

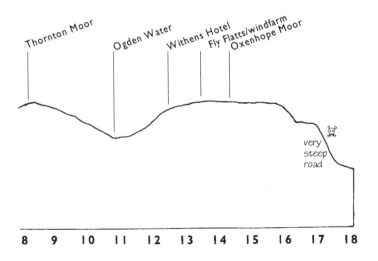

Thornton Moor   Ogden Water   Withens Hotel   Fly Flatts/windfarm   Oxenhope Moor

very
steep
road

8 9 10 11 12 13 14 15 16 17 18

Oxenhope. Descend past the church and the Bay Horse, and down to a crossroads near the end of the village. Here turn **L** down Station Road to return to the station.

ALONG THE WAY

- <u>Ogden Reservoir</u> has in recent years been renamed Ogden Water, and with this subtle change Yorkshire Water have created a visitor attraction, including an access area featuring woodland walks.
- <u>Ovenden Moor windfarm</u> is, needless to say, a prominent landmark in all moorland views in the district. On leaving the Withens Hotel it is very soon alongside, and an information booth is open to visitors. On the other side of the road is the windswept Warley Moor Reservoir, locally known as Fly Flatts. Its modest depth is such that the great drought of 1995 exposed almost all of its floor.
- <u>Oxenhope</u> is a fine example of what was once a thriving Pennine mill community. The Worth Valley Railway ends here, confirming its original purpose in serving the mills, but the village lets its illustrious neighbour Haworth deal with the tourist hordes. The station features a railway museum. A popular and now famous local event is the annual straw race in July, a colourful pub crawl which is a great charity fundraiser.

Sawood, under Thornton Moor

2

ILKLEY MOOR

START Ilkley　　　　　Grid ref. 115470

DISTANCE COVERED　　27km/16½ miles
(Loop 1 only: 14km/8½ miles　Loop 2 only: 21km/13miles)
On road 19km/11½ miles　　**Off road** 8km/5miles

TIME ALLOWED 3½ hours　　**GRADIENT DIFFICULTY** 3

ACCESS Car White Wells or town centre car parks **Train** Ilkley station.

ORDNANCE SURVEY MAPS
1:50,000 - Landranger 104, Leeds & Bradford
1:25,000 - Pathfinder 671, Keighley & Ilkley

SUGGESTED BREAK Holden Beck ford is a sheltered and quiet spot

SUMMARY
This ride takes you from the Wharfe Valley across the peat moorland of Ilkley Moor to the Aire Valley. The contrast between the relatively quiet Ilkley and the more developed Keighley is what really makes the ride. Though featuring several pretty steep climbs the road over Ilkley Moor is wide and fairly easy. The 'loop' around Rough Holden just below High Moor gives a good opportunity for views down the valley. You will need a fair amount of stamina as the route is relatively long and involves extended steep climbs before you cross and recross Ilkley Moor. But don't worry; all the effort is worth it as you get a sweeping panorama while carefully freewheeling back down into Ilkley.

For alternative shorter routes you may elect to do one of the 'loops'. For Loop 1 after emerging from Bury Lane just go right at the first crossroads and return over the moor. For Loop 2 ignore the bridleway on the left after descending off Ilkley Moor and proceed to the crossroads and go right. Pick up the directions below where shown.

S Starting at White Wells car park off Westwood Drive, coming out of the car park turn **L** along the road. Just in front of the Glenmoor conference centre take a **L**, **¶** as a dead end as the road begins to climb.

The road turns from metalled to a wide rocky track after the steepest part of the climb out. Simply follow this track over the moor top to Cowper's Cross on the right, shortly before the gate onto another metalled road. You are now as close as you will get to the radio mast which came into view on your left some time ago.

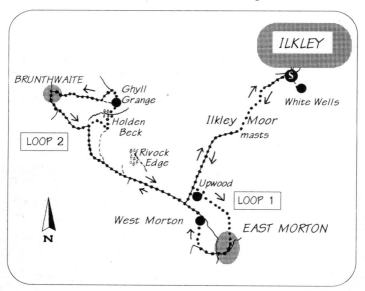

Through the gate you'll enjoy a lovely sweeping descent to a **¶O** on the **L** just before the first settlement on the left. Follow the hardpacked track straight on, passing farm buildings on the right and ignoring the first track left. Part way down the track turns into a grass track and may be very muddy in winter or after heavy rain. Staying on this track, flanked by stone walls either side, it eventually bends right downhill and onto a well made track at a minor crossroads. Come into the back of East Morton and at the T-junction with a road bear **R** into the village.

Follow the road downhill past the Busfeild Arms to a T-junction with the main road and **R.** Follow the road out of the village. Pass the golf course on your left and as it finishes and before the road turns 90 degrees left down Swine Lane look for a small unsignposted **O** on the **R**, just before a small number of houses. On turning into it you will see it marked as Bury Lane. Follow the narrowing track uphill. The main track is obvious and bends left and right into a field just before Dean House Farm. Follow it between the farm buildings and pick up a well made track through West Morton. At the T-junction at the top go **L.**

*LOOP 2 DIRECTIONS ALSO START HERE - FOR LOOP 1 SIMPLY TAKE THE NEXT R BACK OVER THE MOOR. Follow this straight road. It takes you on a level course above the Aire Valley to your left and past two ¶O on the right. Ignore these and shortly after them the road drops and bends round to the right. At a steep left-hand bend take the ¶O to the **R**, through a gate (4km after you joined the road at East Morton).

Refreshment break above Holden Beck

Follow the grass track and note the waymarkers on the stone where the track splits, the blue **O** marker taking you **R**, upfield to a gate and through it. Go straight up this small, narrow field and through the gate facing you at the end. Bear immediately **L** and follow the wall down this tussocky field, with gorse bushes to your right.

Don't worry if the track becomes indistinct here. You're definitely on the right track if you see a big water pipe crossing Holden Beck and swing right, above the beck. The path leads down, underneath the pipe and you take your choice of footbridge or ford and into the opposite field.

The path again becomes indistinct, but follow the wall on the left to the very top, where a yellow waymarker takes you onto what is still a **O**, a hardpacked track and up to Ghyll Grange Farm. In front of the buildings follow the arrow **L** through a gate and around the buildings to a T-junction with a concrete road. Go **R** here and bend through the farm buildings. Just past the big house on your right go **L** off the concrete track up a hardpacked track and into the field at the end.

Follow the wall on your left and **L** onto the concrete track which you hit shortly. This comes immediately to a main road and go **L**, off Lightbank Lane, downhill. Careful on the brakes on this long downhill

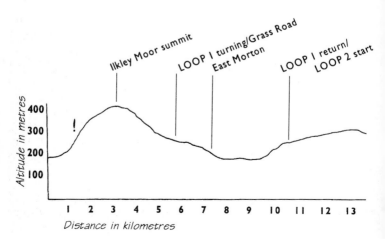

run, taking you through the settlements of High Brunthwaite and Brunthwaite to a T-junction. Bear **L** here onto Hawber Lane and shortly at the next T-junction **L** onto Holden Lane. Stay on this road, soon beginning to climb steeply onto Silsden Road, with the **O**s on your left that you passed earlier. Follow this road until the first crossroads and **L**. You can now retrace your earlier steps over Ilkley Moor and back to your starting point.

ALONG THE WAY

• _White Wells_ The white cottage-type buildings near your starting point at the foot of Ilkley Moor. Possibly the town's most distinctive visitor attraction. Visible from various parts of the town centre near the river, these former open air baths sit commandingly on the slopes of Ilkley Moor. A local squire first exploited the local resource in the mid 1700's and a hydropathic company later added roofs and various other extensions. The baths are now a museum and within easy walking distance of the town centre.

• _Cowper's Cross_ A cowper was a dealer or barterer, and it is likely this is a market cross brought from elsewhere and later made into a true cross.

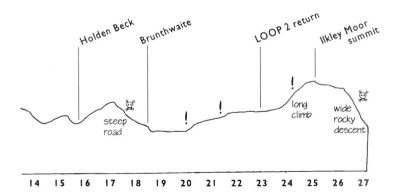

3

HAREWOOD HOUSE

START Horsforth   Grid ref. 236408

DISTANCE 22km/13¾ miles
On road 7km/4½ miles   **Off road** 15km/9¼ miles

TIME ALLOWED 3 hours   **GRADIENT DIFFICULTY** 2

ACCESS Start the route on the quiet country lane leading north from the Brownberries area of Horsforth, running just east of Leeds/Bradford Airport. **Car** Room for a couple of cars off the road at the start, or park in Horsforth. **Train** From Horsforth station on the Harrogate line. Starting point is 3½km north of the station.

ORDNANCE SURVEY MAPS
1:50,000 - Landranger 104, Leeds, Bradford & Harrogate
1:25,000 - Pathfinder 672, Harewood; 683, Leeds

SUGGESTED BREAK Peaceful Wharfe Valley views from the rough track after climbing from the buildings behind Harewood House.

SUMMARY
This route is conveniently near the Leeds/Bradford metropolis and makes quite a comfortable half day ride. The route starts off fairly undramatically taking in a tranquil wooded section. The paths here, after Paul's Pond, are quite reasonable but get very sticky when wet, so are best avoided then. They are quite flat and technically pretty easy. The more dramatic part of the route comes after passing north of Eccup Reservoir as the more frequently wooded landscape takes on more of a rolling grandeur and good views of Harewood House are afforded. The approach to the small village of Weardley leads you above the broad green bottom of the lower Wharfe Valley. After Eccup Reservoir road the paths are generally wide and hardpacked. Gradients shouldn't pose any problem for anyone with a reasonable level of fitness.

24

S The country lane at the start eventually runs north to join a T-junction on Bramhope Moor. The **¶O** is on the **R** coming out of Horsforth and in fact is the only **O** on this road. There was also a **¶** at the roadside indicating the track went to Dean Grange and Nethersprings. Follow the track down the concrete path through the first farm and bear left after the main yard, following the Leeds Country Way marking (yellow owl) downhill. A short, steep downhill section requires good control, then cross over the Harrogate railway line and a small stream, ascending out of this small valley. Pass through a farm, bending round and passing Cookridge cricket club on the right.

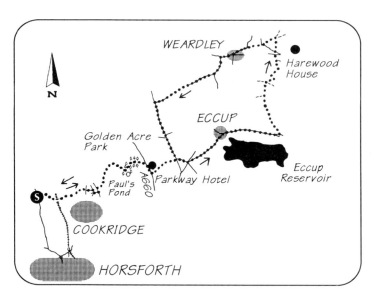

Ignore the **¶O** on the right just after the cricket club and carry straight on the road ahead (Smithy Lane) to the T-junction joining Crag Hill Avenue and **R** here. Turn **L** at the end onto Green Lane and almost immediately **L** again at the T-junction with the main road. Take the next **R** a **¶O** down Pinfold Lane. Follow the lane past the Scout building on the right and through a few houses, then through a gate and into a field, following woods on the left. At the end of this first field follow the blue waymarking and bend **R,** shortly going past a disused building and to a gate at the edge of some woods.

Through the gate look for the blue waymarked track in front of you to the right. Shortly, on coming to a junction of paths by a bank on the right (which hides Paul's Pond), go **L** continuing through the woods and following the line of the small stream on your right that emerges from Paul's Pond. Wend your way through the trees and over the bridge, picking up the waymarking on the other side. This takes you to the southerly edge of the wood. Ignore the larger bridge you may soon see on the left - stick to the path at the edge of the woods on the right. The bridge may look tempting but leads to a footpath going through Breary Marsh Wood, an SSSI (Site of Special Scientific Interest).

Follow the chosen route out of the woods and over a grass track to the A660. Go **R** and look for the **O L** down the side of the Parkway Hotel on the opposite side of the road. Follow the rough path parallel to a lakeside walk behind the hotel and down a nice, wide hardpack track to the road at the end. Go straight across the road onto King Lane to the next junction of Five Lane Ends. Here pick up the **L ¶** *Eccup treatment works* (Eccup Moor Road), not the most immediate left.

Remain on this road, through the hamlet of Eccup on your left and to the control barrier at the start of the water authority road above Eccup Reservoir. Continue past the *no entry* and water authority signs down this road until the junction at the end, facing the treatment works. In front of the works look out for the **¶O L** which turns you 90 degrees, to go north towards Harewood House.

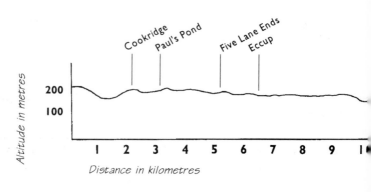

26

Follow this good quality track past the first ¶O to the left and past a farm enter woods to a junction of several O. To your L are two ¶ *Ebor Way*. Don't take the most immediate left, but the next one which bends **steeply** downhill and right. At the bottom of the drop pick up a ¶O to the L and past a disused building on the right and into the ornamental gardens behind Harewood House, with great views of the rear of this stately home.

Follow the main track straight on after coming into the grounds and to a T-junction where a O is waymarked with a blue arrow to the L. Ascend past a brick wall on the right to a cluster of buildings. Coming into the buildings ignore all minor turnings to the right and left and go through the buildings straight up the hill. Pass over two cattle-grids to a O junction on the brow of the hill above Wharfedale.

At this junction two O lead off on good concrete paths to the right. Ignore these and cut back L on a ¶O through a gate onto a rough track. There are good views over the Wharfe from this track; a good opportunity for a break. At the end of this track emerge R onto a small road and over a bridge. First left is marked as a private road but next L takes you through a narrow strip of woodland to the road at the back of Weardley. Although this track appears to be marked as a footpath on entering it, you'll discover it's a ¶O at the Weardley end.

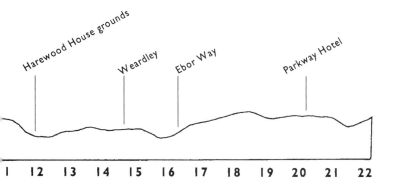

Springtime near Weardley

Bear **L** through the village and at the first set of crossroads coming out, stick **R** (¶ *Arthington 2¼*) and **L** at the next turning, just before the unusual gate lodge to the Rawden Hill residence. Descend and after two houses take the first **R,** marked only as a dead end. Follow the main track past a farm on the right and through the gate - no ¶ on this section. It becomes clear at the next gate you are following the Ebor Way.

This track comes to the main road at Bank Top farm. Go **L** here. Follow the road past left and right turns and opposite the next left turn look for the ¶**O R**. You have now rejoined the track you came out on so retrace your steps to the Parkway Hotel and through woods and farms, back to your starting point.

ALONG THE WAY
• <u>Harewood House</u> Dating from 1759. *The exquisite architecture is complemented by Robert Adam interiors and Chippendale furniture. Also look out for the famous bird garden.*
Open: Mar-end Nov, daily 11-5

• <u>The lower Wharfe Valley</u> *Try to pick out the villages of Weeton and Huby on the far banks of the valley and, as you climb onto the Ebor Way, look out for the Harrogate line stretching over the viaduct towards Huby.*

4

THE PLAIN OF YORK

START *Tockwith*   *Grid ref. 465527*

DISTANCE COVERED *24km/15 miles*
On road *9km/5½ miles*   **Off road** *15km/9½ miles*

TIME ALLOWED *2 hours*   **GRADIENT DIFFICULTY** *Easy 1*

ACCESS *Start in Tockwith.* **Car** *Park on the road in the village.* **Train** *Cattal station is 4½km north of Tockwith on the Harrogate-York line.*

ORDNANCE SURVEY MAPS
1:50,000 - Landranger 105, York
1:25,000 - Pathfinder 664, York (West);   673, Tadcaster

SUMMARY
This really is ideal for the novice. The majority of off road tracks are wide and hard. I've done the route a couple of times in spring and although the landscape is largely huge flat fields, there are plenty of trees and fields of oilseed rape that give pleasant colour and variety.

S Just coming into Tockwith from Cowthorpe, take the first ¶O on the **L**, a concrete road. Shortly after passing two houses on the left go **R** down Moor Lane; the friendly sign gives details of a High Court injunction preventing motor vehicles going down the grass track (well used by horses). Join the concrete road at the other end and **R** to rejoin the main road at the end of Tockwith by a T-junction.

Go **L** at this T-junction and shortly **R** down a ¶O *Jorvic Way & Bilton church*. Follow this well made track past farm buildings, ignoring the first split left, by allotments. Continue more or less in a straight line over fields and into the 'back' of Bilton to the main road. Cross over the main road past the church, ¶ *Bilton village only, ¼*. Proceed through the heart of the village, bending left then right and ignoring minor turns to the left.

29

Pass the Chequers Inn on the right and onto a well made **O**. Follow the track to Nova Scotia Wood and pass it on the right. Just after turning away from the woods follow the track right, through gateposts by a yellow waymarker. Come to a minor T-junction with a concrete road and bear **L,** leading you past Healaugh Grange on the left to a T-junction with the main road.

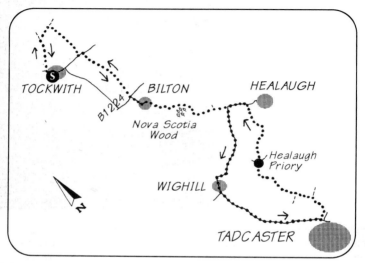

Go **R** onto this road and in just over 2km pass through Wighill village, staying on the main road to the edge of Tadcaster in another 3km. Just after you reach the first buildings look for a ¶**O** onto a hardpacked track on the **L,** just past an antique-looking brick house (beware, the ¶ is on the opposite side of the road, so it's easy to miss). If you see Hudson Way on the left you know you have just gone too far.

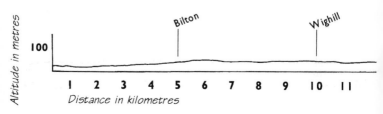

*River Wharfe
above Tadcaster*

Follow this track past residences on the right to a split and **L** (¶ *no cars and motorcycles*). This wide easy track leads to Healaugh Priory on your left. Ignore the private concrete road on the left just past the priory and continue through farm outhouses on the main track. By staying on this and ignoring any gated tracks you will arrive at a T-junction with a road, and Healaugh just to the right. Go **L** onto the road and on the left hand bend turn **R** onto the track by the sign for Healaugh Grange. Follow the track you used earlier to get back to Tockwith on the same route.

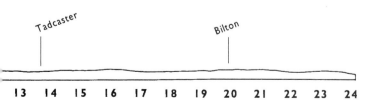

Tadcaster

Bilton

| 13 | 14 | 15 | 16 | 17 | 18 | 19 | 20 | 21 | 22 | 23 | 24 |

5

FULNECK & COCKERS DALE

START Pudsey   Grid ref. 217321

DISTANCE COVERED 15km/9¼ miles
On road 8km/5 miles   **Off road** 7km/4½ miles

TIME ALLOWED 2 hours

GRADIENT DIFFICULTY 2 (the odd grade 3 in places)

ACCESS Start in front of the Bankhouse Inn at the back of Pudsey. **Car**
There is a fair amount of on road parking outside the inn or further up
the road on the main street through the Fulneck Moravian settlement.
(note: it is accessed only from the east). **Train** New Pudsey or Bramley
on the Caldervale line - access to starting point is quite complicated
through Pudsey - see OS map.

ORDNANCE SURVEY MAPS
1:50,000 - Landranger 104, Leeds, Bradford & Harrogate
1:25,000 - Pathfinder 682, Bradford;   682, Leeds

SUGGESTED BREAK The path running through the top of Sykes
Wood looks down over a small stream and contains a fair amount of
wildlife in spring or summer.

SUMMARY
*Although surrrounded by heavily urban areas this run gives you the
impression, in certain places, you are out in the middle of the country,
especially the Sykes Wood section. Much of the rest of the route is a
mix of urban and agricultural use. The route is certainly best tackled,
at least by beginners, in the figure of eight direction intended, as the
two downhill sections at the back of Fulneck are pretty stony, and if
done uphill would be quite a tough proposition. The loop out of*

Cockersdale through Gildersome has been put in specifically to avoid the horribly busy A58 and its lethal lorries. A good half day ride of medium difficulty, conveniently close to urban centres.

Ⓢ LOOP 1: SCHOLEBROOK AND TYERSAL

From the Bankhouse Inn go down Scholebrook Lane, in front and to the right going away from the inn (¶O). At the bridge at the bottom of the descent bear **L** uphill, taking you through the middle of Scholebrook Farm. The road becomes tarmaced and at the next T-junction go **R** onto Raikes Lane. At the next T-junction **R** again. Watch out for the next **R** which appears to be signed confusingly as Landscove Avenue. It is in fact Holme Lane which becomes Ned Lane. Stay on this road as it dips and twists, ignoring minor turnings until you come into an area of flats. Take the first **R**, unmarked, which doubles back past signs for Harper's Gate on the right (a farm).

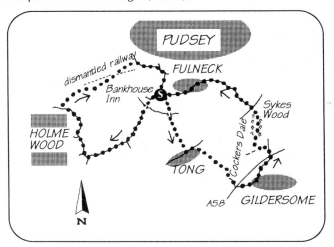

Follow this road which becomes a track, downhill, cutting through a railway embankment and over a stream to a steep climb bringing you onto Smalewell Road. Bear **R** past the Fox & Grapes pub on the right. Continue to the end of Smalewell Road and **R** at the T-junction with the main road. Past the White Cross pub turn **R** up Bankhouse Lane. This brings you past a Sunday School and church back to the Bankhouse Inn.

LOOP 2: THROUGH TONG AND SYKES WOOD

This time bear slightly to the **L** in front of the inn and down Lower Bankhouse, also **¶O**. Carry on between The Bungalow and Newstead House as the path becomes very rocky. Descend to a stream after a golf course on the left. Go over the small footbridge and bear left following the main track up the hill. Eventually join a metalled track and continue to the main road in Tong. **L** onto the main road and just going out of the village look for a **¶O** on the **R** for Springfield Lane.

Pass the private road to Manor Farm on the right and carry on descending on this track to a small stream (Leeds Country Way footpath waymarked off to the left). Carry on the main track to farm buildings, following this track round left becoming metalled. Come out on the main road by the Valley Inn. Go straight across onto New Road and ascend to a T-junction and **L**. In a short while jink **R** onto the main road then immediate **L** onto Back Lane by the Woodcock pub.

Shortly after this turning look for the **O** on the **L** (easy to miss) **¶** as a footpath and **O** to Sykes Wood (also known as Nan Whins Wood), Tong and Fulneck. Shortly on the **R** go through the gate waymarked as a **O** (the main track to the left is a footpath). Follow the main track into the woods above Tong Beck. Ignore a footpath to the right just before passing over a tiny beck. Descend over two sets of wooden steps to the main road.

Go more or less straight across here, uphill into Pudsey. Go past the Weasel pub and shortly after the Boar's Head pub go **L** down Fulneck and into the Moravian settlement. Continue on the road through the school. Go in a straight line ignoring minor turnings, back to the Bankhouse Inn.

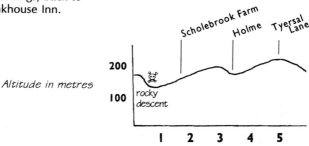

Altitude in metres

Distance in kilometres

At Black Hey Farm, Pudsey

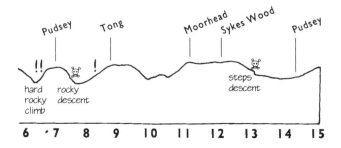

6

SHIBDEN DALE

START Northowram   Grid ref. 112275

DISTANCE   14km/8½ miles
On road   6km/3½ miles   **Off road**   8km/5 miles

TIME ALLOWED 2½ hours   **GRADIENT DIFFICULTY** 3

ACCESS Start in Northowram Green. **Car** The chosen starting point
is wide enough to accommodate on-road parking. **Train** Northowram
is about 4km from Halifax station.

ORDNANCE SURVEY MAPS
1:50,000 - Landranger 104, Leeds, Bradford & Harrogate
1:25,000 - Pathfinder 691, Halifax

SUGGESTED BREAK The viewpoint over Halifax from the back of
Pule Hill is one of my favourite in the whole of West Yorkshire.

SUMMARY
Although this is the shortest route in the book it makes up for this with
its impressively steep gradients. Shibden Dale is a real gem of West
Yorkshire semi-rural landscape, but conveniently close to several
major urban areas. The only off road section in danger of becoming
seriously muddy in the wet is the first section you encounter, leading
off the A644.

From the viewpoint behind Pule Hill look out for numerous landmarks; the Wainhouse Tower on the far side of Halifax, Stoodley Pike
to the right of this in the far distance, and Emley Moor way to the left
with Holme Moss masts somewhere in between, as well as numerous
moors.

S Take the road leading north away from the main road through Northowram towards the hospital. Follow it past the Yew Tree pub on the right to split **L** down Landemere Sike. Shortly take the first **R** up Tan House Lane and uphill to meet the A644 at the T-junction. **L** here along the **busy road** and shortly after the minor road to the right go **L** onto an unmarked **O**. There are good views here across the top of Shibden Head to the right.

Follow what becomes a mud/earth track across a minor track and at the first fork bear **L** and immediately through a gate. Follow the track to the end past old outhouses on the left. Go through a gate to the road and **R**. The road takes you downhill to a T-junction. Go **R** onto Blake Hill End and follow it through a small settlement as the road bends sharp left past a rough track on the right. Follow the road (Paddock Road) until it bears **R** then look for a track (no ¶) **L** down Addersgate.

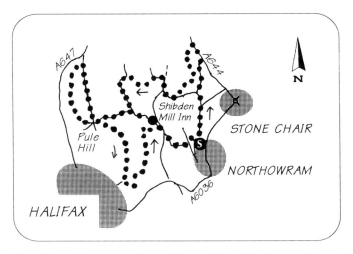

Follow the track as it goes through the middle of the farm and through a gate where the track narrows. Carry on to a T-junction at the end and **L** down a steep, rocky track to join a road at the bottom. Swing round left and follow Shibden Dale bottom with a stream below on your right. An easy downhill 'coast' brings you to a T-junction with a bridge. Go **R** over the bridge, starting to climb steeply up the other side of the dale.

Climb steeply coming into the small settlement of Pule Hill on a cobbled road. At the crossroads at the top go **R** past the Red Lion pub onto the main road. Pass the Starving Rascal pub on the left then various other buildings. Shortly after the quarry entrance on the left go **L** onto an unmarked **O** onto a narrow track by tall iron fencing. Continue on here to a rough T-junction with a grass road at the end and **L** to go behind the quarry, then a farm, then a landfill site.

Keep son the main track straight ahead, coming to the great viewpoint on the right side of the track atop a crag. After this the track drops to join the main road. Continue on the road to the crossroads you previously exited from. Go straight across and immediately look for a **¶O** on the **R** down Hag Lane, with the Sportsman Inn to the right. Follow a rocky path past a small copse of trees to the right to split and bear **L**. At the next split ignore right and carry on under the pylons. After a house on the right you come to a three way split; go immediate **L**. Follow it downhill onto a metalled road (Jerwood Hill Road) and at the T-junction go **L** onto a track; unsigned **O**.

Follow the track through the woods emerging into the car park of Shibden Mill Inn. Cross the car park to the road and go **R** uphill. Climb steeply to the first crossroads and straight across onto Howes Lane. Shortly after the climb levels out come into the back of Northowram to a T-junction and go **L**. Take the first rough track on the **R** through two concrete posts and downhill past a school on the left. Follow it to the end of Baxter Lane and go **L** up Northowram Green to return to the starting point.

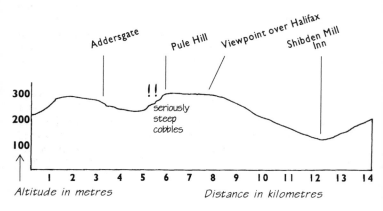

Altitude in metres   *Distance in kilometres*

UPTON & BADSWORTH

START *East Hardwick*   *Grid ref. 463185*

DISTANCE *19km/12 miles*
On road *6km/3½ miles*   **Off road** *13km/8½ miles*

TIME ALLOWED *1½ hours*   **GRADIENT DIFFICULTY** *1*

ACCESS *Start from the main street.* **Car** *The main road through East Hardwick is wide enough to park on.* **Train** *Use one of the three stations in Pontefract. East Hardwick is 3½km from the town centre.*

MAP
1:50,000 - Landranger 111, Sheffield & Doncaster
1:25,000 - Pathfinder 704, Hemsworth & Askern

SUMMARY
Although this route may not have the best scenery of all the routes, it's certainly one of the easiest in the book. It is distinguished not only by its relatively short length and flatness but also by the large proportion of the route that is on excellent quality bridleway. You only have to encounter a couple of bumpy fields and most other off road riding is on good hardpacked, well drained tracks. Generally the route is an ideal beginner's or younger rider's route on which to learn the basics of control.

S From the main street head back to the T-junction with the A639 and go **L** onto it. Shortly take the first ¶**O** on the **R**. Follow this hardpacked track left at the very minor split by the house as you enter onto the **O**, and down the narrow path following the track to a road and straight across onto a ¶**O**. Follow the concrete road past a water service station on the left and continue straight on the hardpacked track to join a road.

Go straight across the road through a small gate and across the field on the obvious path, past Rogerthorpe Manor on the left. Into the next field and follow this bumpy path towards the water beacon, down and up hill, past the woods on the left. Emerge at a T-junction in Upton and **L** onto the road. Follow this road to a T-junction and **L** again. Follow this road through Upton for 2km, until a sign shows a **O** coming from the **R**, just after a right hand bend and downhill stretch.

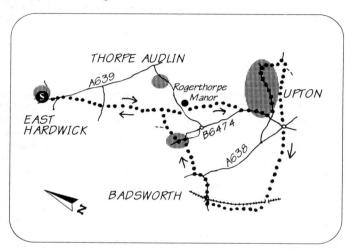

Very shortly on this **O** there is a split; a smaller track goes left through an old brick bridge but stay straight on the main track. Follow this disused railway line for about 1½km and through a gate to reach a

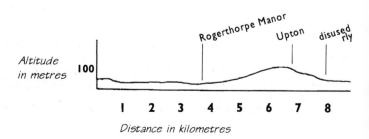

Altitude in metres **100**

Distance in kilometres

roundabout. Stay on the main track, which follows more or less a straight line. At the roundabout ignore the first left for the A638 Doncaster road, and take the second **L.**

Immediately after turning off there is an unsignposted track to your **R**, down a steep drop back onto the disused railway line. If you want a good shower here the downhill section provides good speed through the water! Follow this track for another 1½ km to the railway bridge. Go over the left hand bridge onto a wide grass track and right in about 30 metres on the **R** down a smaller, unsignposted grass track to a field. Go **L** along the edge of this field to a blue and yellow waymarked log in the corner. Follow this field edge and **L** in the corner. Go straight on at the track crossroads, past the railway bridge on your right.

This **O** runs parallel to the railway until meeting the road where you turn **R**. At the T-junction with the A638 go **L** and immediate **R ¶** *Badsworth ½.* Coming into Badsworth turn first **L** at a minor crossroads down Nineveh Lane and second **R** down Grove Lane. At the farm buildings there is a split. Bear **R** as the track to the left is marked private, no access. At the end of this track go **L** at the **O** T-junction. You can now retrace your route out, going straight over the next road and **L** on the A639 back into East Hardwick on the **R.**

LEGAL NOTE: AT THE TIME OF WRITING THE DISUSED RAILWAY LINE RUNNING FROM UPTON TO THE MAIN RAILWAY WAS WIDELY REGARDED AS BEING A PERMISSIVE BRIDLEWAY THOUGH NOT RECORDED ON MAPS. IT IS PART OF WAKEFIELD COUNCIL'S SCHEME OF PROVIDING CYCLE ROUTES IN THE AREA. AFTER FORMAL NEGOTIATIONS IT SHOULD BE MARKED AS A CYCLE ROUTE. THE COUNCIL CURRENTLY USE A WHITE BIKE ON A CIRCULAR BLUE BACKGROUND TO INDICATE THIS.

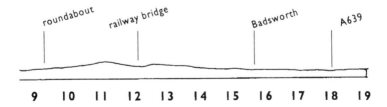

8

WOOLLEY EDGE

START *Sandal Castle* *Grid ref. 336182*

DISTANCE *26km/16 miles (28km/17½ miles with 'railway' start)*
On road *17km/10½ miles* **Off road** *9km/5½ miles*

TIME ALLOWED *4 hours* **GRADIENT DIFFICULTY** *1, occasionally 2*

ACCESS *Start from Sandal Castle.* **Car** *Free car park opening at 9.30am; closing time varies (shown on the entrance gate).* **Train** *Sandal & Agbrigg station (see Directions for this start).*

ORDNANCE SURVEY MAPS
1:50,000 - Landranger 110, Sheffield & Huddersfield **or**
Landranger 111, Sheffield & Doncaster
1:25,000 - Pathfinder 703, Wakefield South

SUGGESTED BREAK *The car park at Woolley Edge gives excellent views over the Pennines and is a local beauty spot.*

SUMMARY
This medium length route gives you great views over the area between Wakefield and Barnsley. It starts off quietly enough taking in the historic site of Sandal Castle and leaving the rich suburbia of south-east Wakefield to take a look at the remains of the now disused Wakefield - Barnsley canal. The pretty village of Notton prepares you for the even prettier delights of Woolley village, packed full of beautiful houses. It still retains its 'village feel' centred, as it is, around a green, parish hall and church.

The route purposely takes you around the Woolley Edge plateau so you get fine panoramas, and from the various lookouts you will be able to see the Pennines to the west, Wakefield and Barnsley and numerous power stations to the plain of York in the east. The route winds up, as it began, passing through quiet woods at the back of Newmillerdam Country Park before a stretch of road back to your starting point. There aren't any 'killer' sections here but good technique is required on the narrow field bridleways coming away from Woolley village, especially after rain when they may be muddy. All in all a good mix of scenery: woods, villages and fine views sum up the character of this area perfectly.

S From the car park go **L** onto the road. Follow this until very shortly meeting a crossroads with Castle Road and **L** onto the unmetalled road. (**Railway start:** from Sandal & Agbrigg station, come out onto Agbrigg road and **L** until meeting the A61 Barnsley road. Go **L** and immediate **R** (after the no entry turning), onto Sandal Avenue - you must cross over the pavement as the road is a cul-de-sac with a wall at the end of it at this point. Go **R** at the T-junction at the end of Sandal Avenue. At the crossroads at the end of Castle Road go straight over onto an unmetalled road.)

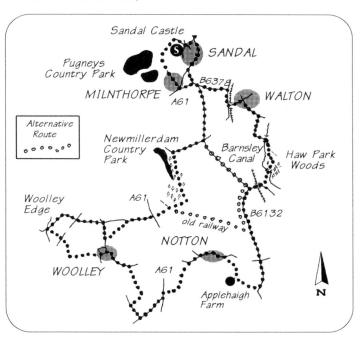

Follow this unmetalled road ignoring any minor turnings. The track curves round almost 180 degrees, keeping Sandal Castle on your left all the time. Just before leaving the houses on your right you cross over a small track crossroads - the right going down the side of some houses and the left over a field towards the castle (footpath). Bend round in a large curve to the left and downhill to a split in the path going **L**.

There is now a great view of the castle atop a rising field as you cycle along the path at its bottom, having just passed a good view of the Pugneys straight ahead of you (the Pugneys are two small lakes used as a local boating and leisure reserve). Continuing on this track past farm buildings on the right, onto a metalled road past Milnthorpe Drive on the left. At the end of this road you meet the A61 again and straight across down Carr Lane - another 'dead end' with concrete bollards at the end. At the end of Carr Lane go **R** onto Chevet Lane then shortly **L** down Walton Station Lane.

Another brief spell of farmland brings you to a T-junction with Greenside. Go **R** into then first **L** down the Shay taking you over a railway bridge. Continue for about 100 metres looking out for The Balk just before a war memorial and go **R** down here. Continue on this road - there is a left you can take ¶ *Waterton Park Golf Club* which takes you to Walton Hall; you can follow this road to the hotel at the end if you want a look at this fine building situated on its own island in a lake. You will have to turn round and come back to the road as it's a dead end, even for cyclists. The Balk passes speed de-restriction signs; go past a footpath on the right and to a junction where there is a footpath to the right. Follow what is now a rough track round the left hand bend to the bridge over the old canal, amidst woods and a couple of luxury residences.

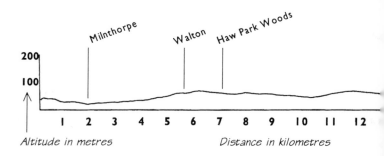

Altitude in metres   Distance in kilometres

Follow the path by the side of the canal. It can get very muddy going here in winter so you'll need all your skill to keep going through the sticky patches! This **O** splits into two at the end of a high wall. Bear **R**, sticking by the canal for a short while and heading through another sticky patch towards Haw Park Woods. On reaching the wooden fence on the edge of the woods the **O** doesn't enter them and the track diverts down the **R** side of the woods following the edge of a field. After a short while follow the track through a corner of the woods to a small bridge, recrossing the canal.

Just over the small bridge carry on the main track through the woods; a good but short, bumpy section. BEWARE! At the end of this short section the track goes up and meets the canal on the other side - you can't see it until you come over the rise so watch your speed to avoid a ducking! Bear **R** on meeting the canal, keeping it on your left. At the end of the canal look out for a small **R** off the main track, just after a concrete post on the right (otherwise unmarked). Follow this through the trees at the edge of the wood to where it exits at the road. Take a **R** onto this road.

(Note - Wakefield Council's Countryside Service may be marking the bridleway from the road and generally tidying up the last section of it to make it more obvious. Also note that the bridleway is shown on maps after Clay Royd bridge as going into a field. This is not the case; follow it through the woods as instructed above).

Pass under the railway bridge to the B6132 T-junction and go **L** ¶ *Royston*. A longer road section brings you to a crossroads, going straight over past the Oliver Twist pub on the right onto Bleakley Lane. Just after the sign advising that you're now in the Barnsley District

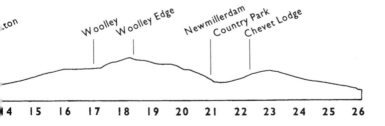

Council area, and before a sign for Royston, look out for an unmarked **O** to the **R** of a retaining wall for a disused railway embankment. Drop down onto this partly surfaced track, eventually coming to a split. Applehaigh Farm is on the left so go **R** at this split over a tiny bridge, past the small woods on your right.

This turns into a metalled road, so follow it into Notton proper, over the village green and past the post office. **L** on the main road takes you through the village centre and on approaching farm buildings at the end of the village look for a **L** down Keeper Lane. Follow through open country to the A61 and **L** then immediate **R**.

Continue up the hill and just as you get to the brow take the first road on the **R**. Shortly on this road take the first unsignposted track **R** down to a main track, and bending left to go through farm buildings to the road. **L** will take you to the village of Woolley and bear first **L** when you hit the green. Follow this road to a dead end sign, Mollyhurst Lane, and down here. The road becomes a track. Pass through a gate and to the corner of the first field. A footpath continues straight on at the corner but stay in this field bending right.

Pass through another gate to Intake Lane. Cross here, the **O** continues on the other side of the road. Cross the field you've just entered, keeping the copse of trees on your right and pick up a small gate at the other side of the field. A short, steepish descent leads to a crossroads at Woolley Edge - take the most immediate **R** as you emerge.

Continue on this road over the first set of crossroads and then **R** down Water Lane, ¶ *Woolley Hall College*. Next **L** down Parson Lane brings you to a T-junction; go **R**. On meeting the A61 look for the entrance to a **O** down a narrow concrete path directly opposite you. Initially you pass an industrial unit which is fenced off on your left. Crossing over a disused railway bridge, go **R** down the main track by the Newmillerdam Country Park sign.

ALTERNATIVE ROUTE: Immediately on passing over the disused railway bridge there is a further path suitable for cycles. This takes you along the top of the disused railway line (embankment) and adds just over 2km to the overall route length. On crossing the bridge go *immediate* **R** and eventually you recognise you are on top of an old embankment. Follow this track until you meet the main road at the second bridge (the first bridge is footpath only), the B6132 and go **L** here. Ignore the smaller lane here where you emerge and look for what is obviously the main road at the end of it. This road joins the original route in about 3km at a crossroads. Go straight on and follow directions below.

If not following the alternative route, carry on down the hill on a fast, broad section ignoring any minor turnings and over a small bridge (the stream feeds into Newmillerdam). At the junction just after the bridge follow the main track as it bends round **L**. At the first fork, left is marked by a 'no cycling' post (you may want to dismount and follow this path for a look at the southern end of the beautiful Newmillerdam). The route follows the **R** at this split going uphill. After a short climb ignore another 'no cycling' track on the left and continue on to exit the woods, through some old gateposts and into a large field.

The narrow earth track is obvious from here and has been carefully preserved by the farmer who has ploughed either side of it. You should have no problems following this nice, easy path which dissects the field and meets the 'lodge' (now a private residence) at the other side. Go **R** after leaving the field onto Lodge Lane and to the next cross-roads, going **L** onto the B6132. The alternative route joins at this crossroads - it comes straight down the B6132. Follow this road for 2km, mainly downhill to the T-junction with the A61.

To return to the train station go **R** onto the main road and follow it until Agbrigg Road on the **R** shortly after Sandal Magna church. This brings you to the station on the **R.**

To return to Sandal Castle jink **R** then immediate **L** at this crossroads onto Manygates Lane. This road brings you to the castle on your **L.**

ALONG THE WAY
• _The Barnsley Canal_ This quiet backwater once stretched all the way to Barnsley, and Barnsley coal was exchanged for Wakefield food supplies. It is now disused and in places infilled. It has been partly recolonised by nature and it makes a beautiful ride.

• _Walton Hall_ Not directly on the route but the short detour described in the directions will take you to this fine hotel building. It is the former home of Charles Waterton, a naturalist who effectively created a country park within the grounds for the public. Note the grounds are now private but you can get a good view over the house and grounds from the access road.

47

• _Sandal Castle_ Dating back to the Norman conquest of the north of England, these crumbling ruins sit in a commanding position on high ground and were once the site of buildings that were a testament to the power of factions competing for the throne of England. The plan below shows the main features of the main castle buildings as they would have been after its enlargement in the thirteenth century. After military conquest by Norman nobles it became a royal tax gathering and administration centre.

Richard of York was killed here by Lancastrians at the battle of Wakefield in 1463 and Richard III subsequently rebuilt the castle into a major northern stronghold. The building was all but destroyed by the military bombardment during a siege by Roundheads and was one of the last Royalist strongholds to survive. It remained in decrepit state and was partially covered with earth by victorious Parliamentarians to prevent its reuse by Royalists. Today's remains were finally uncovered and restored during the 1960's.

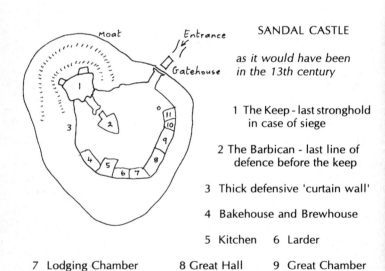

SANDAL CASTLE

_as it would have been
in the 13th century_

1 The Keep - last stronghold
   in case of siege

2 The Barbican - last line of
   defence before the keep

3 Thick defensive 'curtain wall'

4 Bakehouse and Brewhouse

5 Kitchen   6 Larder

7 Lodging Chamber   8 Great Hall   9 Great Chamber

10 Privy Chamber   11 Constable's Lodging

9

HOWELL WOODS

START *Howell Woods* *Grid ref. 433099*

DISTANCE COVERED *26km/16 miles*
On road *13km/8 miles* **Off road** *13km/8 miles*

TIME ALLOWED *3½ hours* **GRADIENT DIFFICULTY** *1/2*

ACCESS *Start at Howell Woods.* **Car** *Free car park.* **Train** *Moorthorpe station on the Wakefield Line is about 3½km from the starting point.*

ORDNANCE SURVEY MAPS
1:50,000 - Landranger 111, Sheffield & Doncaster
1:25,000 - Pathfinder 704, Hemsworth & Askern
716, Doncaster & Dearne

SUMMARY
Howell Woods are beautiful former estate woods under the control and management of Doncaster Council's Countryside Service. They contain good, wide tracks which make for easy biking. However the woods are also very popular with walkers and horseriders and the tracks can become very muddy in winter. Permissive use by cyclists was originally restricted to April-October, but all year use is now permitted. In order to stop excessive path erosion, however, please respect their condition in winter. Other off road sections are generally of good quality, and the gently rolling countryside makes this a good intermediate section, with any steeper climbs being on the road.

S Leave the car park by the right hand track into the woods by advisory/prohibitive signs for horseriders/motorcyclists. Very shortly take the smaller track off **L** before coming to a bench on the left. Follow this downhill and round the bottom of a fishpond taking the first turning off **L**. At the first fork by a seat go **L**. At the next complicated junction ignore the first right and left and bear **R** at a fork.

Follow the main track downhill over small steps to a wide grassy firebreak and **R** uphill. At the top of the firebreak go **R** onto the main track then at the first split go **L** onto a smaller track, running parallel to a field on the left. Continue on this track back to the car park and exit to go **R** to the main road. Go **R** here bringing you into South Kirkby. Take the **R** before the Old Mill pub and downhill. At a left hand bend take an unsignposted track on the **R.** Follow the track through field edges, twisting left then right downhill to a small bridge over a stream. Follow the main track uphill to join a rutted track. Ignore the first right and continue under pylons on the main track.

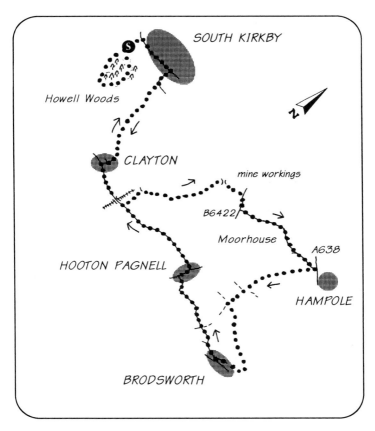

At the major junction in the back of Clayton village pick up a tarmac road, ignoring the track to the right and two to the left (also ¶ as footpaths). Carry on through the village ignoring Chapel Hill on the right, to the main road and **L** ¶ *Hooton Pagnell & Doncaster*. After a downhill over the railway bridge go **L** onto a ¶**O** following the field-side. Pass through a small gate and follow the next field-side to a track T-junction and **R**. Pass over the crossroads where Frickley Hall estate office is to the right and look for the next **L** ¶**O** after going over a cattle-grid.

Head straight along this track as the mine workings come into view ahead of you. Meet the T-junction just in front of the brick bridge and go **R** under the bridge, to a T-junction with the main road and **R** again. Just after passing through an old railway embankment go **L** down Moorhouse Lane ¶ *Moorhouse*. Pass through the small village of Moorhouse continuing on this road until seeing the byway ¶ on the **R**, just after passing under pylons; the byway takes you back under the pylons. Follow the byway south to pass dense woods on your left and ignore the rough track right just after them.

At the next 'mini-crossroads' take a ¶**O L** off the byway as the path leads into the back of Rat Hill Farm. Just through the farm bear **R** on a track. Shortly as the main track bends right take a ¶**O L**. Ignore the next ¶**O** to the right over the field, staying on the main track. At a fork, with a view of the church spire ahead, bear **R**. Coming into farm buildings bear immediate **R** through a gate past a house on the right and bend left past a wall.

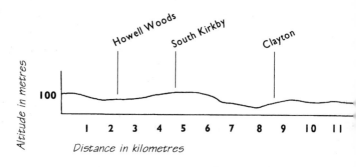

Wakefield from Sandal Castle (previous ride)

Join the tarmac road in the back of Brodsworth and continue to the main road. Go **R** and follow the main road for about 2km to a T-junction and **R** into Hooton Pagnell. Take the first minor split **L** in the village and follow the road downhill. Eventually you will recognise this as the road leading from Clayton. Coming into Clayton take the **R** down Hall Brig. From here it is simply a matter of recognising the route you took on the way out, through the fields and back through South Kirkby to Howell Woods.

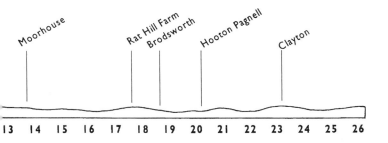

10

THE DOVE VALLEY TRAIL

START *Worsborough Country Park*   *Grid ref. 352034*

DISTANCE COVERED *20km/12½ miles*
On road *7km/4¼ miles*   **Off road** *13km/8¼ miles*

TIME ALLOWED *2½ hours*   **GRADIENT DIFFICULTY** *1/2*

ACCESS Car *It is possible to use the car park at Worsborough Country Park (50p for up to 4 hours at time of writing).* **Train** *The start of the trail is about 3km south of Barnsley's central station. You could also pick up the Dove Valley Trail just north of Wombwell. This would add 8km to the route described.*

ORDNANCE SURVEY MAPS
1:50,000 - Landranger 110, Sheffield & Huddersfield
1:25,000 - Pathfinder 715, Barnsley & Penistone

SUGGESTED BREAK *The minor road leading to Eastfield is very quiet, with good views.*

SUMMARY
The Dove Valley Trail which makes up much of this route is in fact part of SUSTRANS' Trans-Pennine trail. This is the brainchild of this charity and when fully completed will run a total of 240km from Liverpool to Hull. As you can see from the completed Dove Valley section the path is generally even and of really excellent quality compared to the poor or non-existent surfaces of some bridleways. See 'useful addresses' to find out more about the charity's projects.

The remainder of the route takes you through the fairly gentle hills south of the Dove Valley, mainly on very quiet minor roads. The bridleway going through fields at Stainborough Fold is a good example of one that should be used regularly to stop it falling into disuse and its barely visible path disappearing altogether. This short *field section is the only part or the route that is even vaguely difficult and requiring a little off road skill. Overall the route is excellent for those not confident enough to tackle a true off road route, but wishing to gain skills and progress to more difficult routes; it's also a nice, easy half day training ride for those more experienced who don't feel like exerting themselves!*

S Pick up the Dove Valley Trail where it joins the A61 heading south out of Barnsley, through Worsborough. On the A61 from Sheffield to Barnsley you'll see the entrance on your **L** shortly after the parking area for Worsborough Country Park, and immediately before Vernon Road and the Ship Inn. Although unsignposted the trail is easily picked up through red metal gates, which are a constant feature as it crosses or joins tracks and roads.

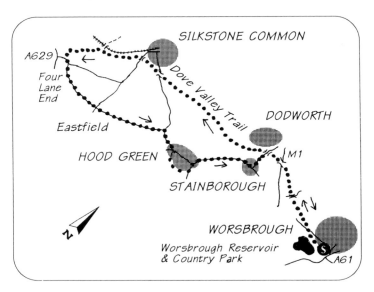

Simply follow the obvious smooth surfaced asphalt track for the whole of the route to its terminus shortly after the village of Silkstone Common. You can use the following landmarks to measure your progress on the route:-
* Across a minor road just after Worsborough Reservoir on your left.
* Through red gates, over a small dirt track before crossing over M1.

55

* Cross over a minor road going into Silkstone Common, seen to the right.
* Shortly after this is a series of two tunnels. The second is long and dark and quite good fun! It's generally flat but watch out for concrete rises in the middle. There is a link path signed avoiding the tunnels if you want.
* Shortly after this the trees close in on the path then the path splits. The Trans-Pennine trail is waymarked left up a well made path and the path that continues to go under a bridge is clearly disused.

At the top of the track bear **L** down a track, away from the bridge immediately on your right. Follow it through farm buildings and bend left on the main track to a road T-junction.

Go **L** at this junction then very shortly take a **R** down a very minor road just past the small group of houses on the right. Follow down and up hill, going over a crossroads from Hopping Lane onto Eastfield Lane. Through the small settlement of Eastfield to a T-junction. **R** here onto Baggerwood Lane and over a small stream to climb through the beautiful Bagger Wood to a T-junction at the main road through Hood Green. **R** then immediate **L** down Greno View, just past a small war memorial on the left.

Round the corner take the **¶O R** and continue to farm houses on the right and the first bungalow on the left. **BEWARE NAVIGATION TRICKY - FOLLOW DIRECTIONS CAREFULLY HERE!** After the

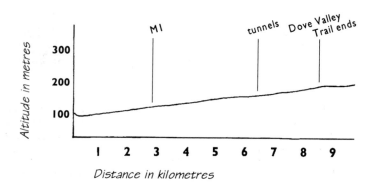

bungalow on the left and the long barn wall on the right look for a gate in the hedge. This O is not ¶ but is faintly marked on the gate. Go L through this gate into a field. Note it is easy to miss this gate and you should beware of a O further on at Lower Fold Farm. If you see these you have gone too far! In the field follow the right hand edge; the track was faintly visible on my visit but may be less so with the growth of crops. Follow to the corner at the bottom and bend left uphill again following the edge of the field. Shortly look for a gate on the **R** into the next field and head down its right edge, keeping the woods on the right. Hit the dirt track at the bottom bearing **R** to a T-junction with the road.

Go **L** onto this road and climb to a T-junction in Hood Green. Go **R** here ¶ Barnsley and Wentworth Castle education centre, onto Lowe Lane. Pass Wentworth Castle (also education centre) on the top of the hill and downhill. Go **L** at the first minor crossroads onto Gilroyd Lane, ¶ Gilroyd and Dodworth. Follow the main road uphill to Gilroyd Bridge; the small row of houses on the right before the bridge bears this name.

Take a **L** down an unsignposted dirt track just before the bridge. This runs into the Dove Valley Trail after a short while by red gates on the right. Loop back **R** onto the trail and simply follow the main track back to your starting point at the A61.

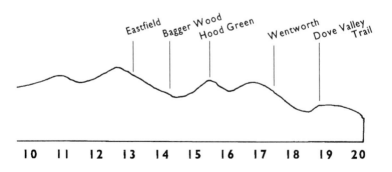

11

MELTON WOOD

START *Sprotborough*   *Grid ref. 533023*

DISTANCE *19km/12 miles*
On road *5km/3 miles*   **Off road** *14km/9 miles*

TIME REQUIRED *2½ hours*   **GRADIENT DIFFICULTY** *2*

ACCESS *Directions start from Sprotbrough.* **Car** *park in Sprotbrough*
Train *Dearne, Conisborough and Doncaster are all possible starting
points. From the first two, the route can be picked up by reference to
the OS Landranger map. From Doncaster station the route is best
started from Sprotbrough.*

ORDNANCE SURVEY MAPS
1:50,000 -Landranger 111, Sheffield & Doncaster
1:25,000 -Pathfinder 716, Doncaster & Dearne

SUGGESTED BREAK *Fine views and stopping places on the second
stretch of bridleway overlooking Barnburgh after 7km/4 miles. Melton
Woods (13km/8 miles) are also very pretty.*

SUMMARY
*Although most of the Doncaster area is extremely flat this route takes
advantage of the small natural ridge above Barnburgh and the Dearne
Valley. Despite this, the flattest part of the route, the very first stretch
of bridleway coming out of Sprotborough (which is also the last
homeward leg) was the most difficult part of the route when I cycled
it in late March. This was due to the fact that farmers had recently
ploughed the fields and the bridleways over the centre of them were
extremely bumpy, not helped further by frequent use by horses.*

*Going through the village of Marr you may want to dismount and
'pavement push' past this busy main road (lots of industrial traffic) for
the short distance until the turning for Mexborough. The flat section*

gives no hint of the more dramatic landscape that can be viewed at the start of the second section of bridleway. Conveniently the countryside service has waymarked the bridleways at some dubious junctions using a blue arrow on a yellow background.

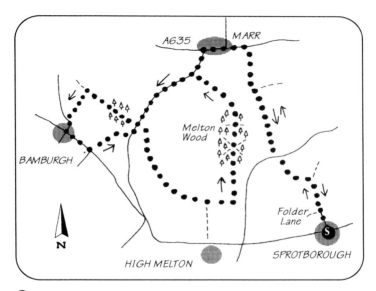

S   On the road leading out of Sprotborough towards High Melton look for Folder Lane heading north off this road. The end of Folder Lane bends left and turns into a gravel road. The **O** is waymarked straight on, on a compacted mud path. This path leads to a split at the edge of small woods where you go **L**, following waymarking and keeping the woods on your right. Just after the edge of the woods bear **R** and the track becomes rougher then narrower. Another waymarker directs you onto a minor road. Go **L** on hitting this road and immediate **R** onto another field track ¶ *Marr*.

A waymarker directs you over the first couple of fields. Split off **L** at the next junction, heading straight for the church in Marr which is clearly visible (the main track bends round right). On reaching the main A635 running through Marr, go **L** and continue through Marr until a **L** down Blacksmiths Lane ¶ *Mexborough*. Continue on this road for 2km and just after a small rise before the road begins to drop more steeply take a **R**, down a **¶O** and into a small wooded area. There are great views over Barnburgh as you ride along this natural ridge. Shortly after emerging from the trees with a field on the right, split off **L** dropping immediately downhill on the first **¶O**.

The **O** descends quite steeply and may be **extremely** muddy after rain and throughout the winter. It emerges onto a metalled road in Barnburgh. On coming to the main road go **L** and follow this road (High Street) round to a crossroads and go **L**. The road descends and just past a pub on the right take the **¶O** on the **L**. Ascend on this rough path which bends right to a road. Go **L** here and a short way up the hill, approaching the brow, look for a **¶O** on the **R;** this is the point at which you turned off into the woods on the opposite side of the road.

Follow the nice, wide sandstone graveled path, essentially following a large left hand curve. At the first waymarked junction go **L** down the narrower earth path, following a wall on the right, although both possible roads are waymarked **O**. The **O** that continues round to the right on the main track arrives in the pretty village of High Melton - worth a quick look if you have time. The narrow track then jinks 90 degrees left and takes you into the woods. The first junction is a meeting of six roads - head straight across - you will know its the right road if you keep two tracks on your right and two on your left at this major junction.

Go over a small crossroads and emerge into a field. This **O** broadens out into a landrover track and leads to a road. Going **R** onto the road leads back to the A635 where you go **R** through Marr. As you are exiting the village look for the **¶O** that you followed from Sprotborough to Marr. Go **R** onto this **O** and retrace your steps to Sprotborough.

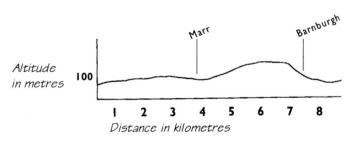

Looking over Barnburgh

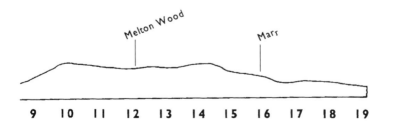

12

ROCHE ABBEY

START   *Roche Abbey*   *Grid ref. 543902*

DISTANCE   *21km/13 miles*
On road   *8km/5 miles*   **On road**   *13km/8 miles*

TIME ALLOWED   *2½ hours*

GRADIENT DIFFICULTY   *1 (with the odd grade 2 climb)*

ACCESS   *Start from the abbey car park.* **Car**   *Signposted from the A634 between Maltby and Stone village.* **Train**   *Unfortunately the area isn't well served by train. Nearest station is Kiveton Park between Sheffield and Worksop.*

ORDNANCE SURVEY MAPS
1:50,000 - Landranger 111, Sheffield & Doncaster
1:25,000 - Pathfinder 727, Rotherham
*   744, Aughton & Carlton in Lindrick*

SUMMARY
The starting point is the small valley housing the beautiful Roche Abbey. You can walk to it from the car park, though an entrance fee is payable to see it close up. It is in the care of English Heritage.

In spring the quiet pale-stoned villages of Letwell and Firbeck are full of flowers, as people in this part of the world seem to have a passion for immaculately tidy and pretty gardens. These villages are entirely in keeping with the well manicured countryside surrounding them. If you don't fancy the drama and effort of Dales and Pennine peaks why not head for the gentle pleasures of this rich agricultural landscape? Some of the tracks between fields are evidently used by horses and this may make them a little bumpy in the dry or sticky in the wet. There are however plenty of easy road sections and this is certainly one of the easier rides featured.

S Wheel bikes over the track away from the car park alongside the beck on the left (this is a footpath), to a minor road, and go **L** onto the road. Climb out of a small valley and continue on the minor road under a small bridge with a good view of Laughton en le Morthen church ahead of you. As you arrive in Slade Hooton come to a T-junction and go **L**. Go downhill and under a bridge followed by another climb to a T-junction in Laughton en le Morthen, opposite the post office, and go **L**. Coming out of the village look for the church on the right; the **O** is the rough track on the **L** (¶ easy to miss as it is hidden in trees).

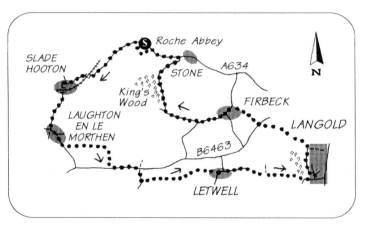

Follow the narrow track between fields bending left then right over a small bridge. On coming to a junction with a well made farm track bear **R** to the road. Go **L** onto the main road then first **R** down Leys Lane, ¶ Dinnington. Take the first ¶**O** on the **L** between fields on a narrow grass track. This runs on in a straight line and becomes bordered by trees and hedges. Follow it uphill past a church to join the main road running through Letwell. Go **L** onto the main road then first **R** off the main road as it bends left. This road becomes a rough track and then meets a tarmac road on a bend where you go straight on.

Go straight over at the next crossroads and bear left onto the main road through a housing estate in Langold as you come out of a small section of woodland. Go first **L** up William Street and **L** at the first crossroads, opposite no entry signs. Follow this road (White Avenue) northwards to its end opposite fenced allotments and bear **L** keeping the allotments on the right. Just round the corner of the woods ahead of you pick up a minor track, with the woods to your left and a field to your right (unsignposted). Ignore any small turnings into the woods then head away from the woods after the Dyscar Woods sign on your left, over the main track ahead of you.

L at the next fork at the corner of field takes you into another series of woods. Follow the main track to the main road. Look for the track directly opposite as you come out of the woods which is a **¶O**. Follow the track downhill and then into the back of Firbeck, staying on the main track through houses to the main road opposite the Black Lion. Go **L** here and carry on New Road past the church on your right and out of the village.

Ignore the first split left, staying on the main road **¶** *Laughton & Rotherham*. Coming to the corner of a large wood turn **R** up Kingswood Lane. Follow this road past the wood on the left and descend to the main road through the edge of Stone village and **L** onto the A634. After a short distance take the first **L** **¶** *Roche Abbey*, descending on a cobbled road back to the car park.

ALONG THE WAY
• <u>Roche Abbey</u> *Beautiful ruins of a Cistercian abbey founded in 1147 in the quiet green valley of the River Ryton. To visit it, leave the car park in the opposite direction from the start of the route.*

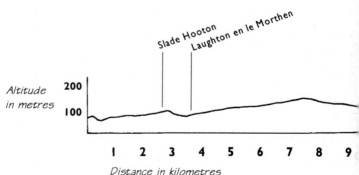

Roche Abbey

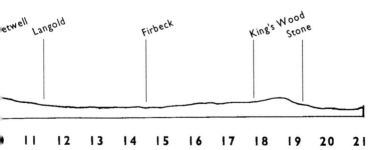

etwell Langold Firbeck King's Wood Stone

11 12 13 14 15 16 17 18 19 20 21

13

WHARNCLIFFE WOODS

START   *Grenoside*   *Grid ref. 332944*

DISTANCE COVERED *15km/9¼ miles*
On road *5km/3 miles*   **Off road** *10km/6¼ miles*

TIME ALLOWED *2½ hours*   **GRADIENT DIFFICULTY** *2*

ACCESS *Start from the main street.* **Car** *Ample parking on the main street.* **Train** *Chapeltown Station on the Penistone and Hallam lines is about 4km from the start of the route. A useful short-cut is the bridleway linking Wood Seats and Grenoside through Grenoside woods.*

ORDNANCE SURVEY MAPS
1:50,000 - Landranger 110, Sheffield & Huddersfield
1:25,000 - Pathfinder 726, Sheffield North & Stocksbridge

SUGGESTED BREAK *A couple of spots below Wharncliffe Crags give great views over the Don Valley, to Wharncliffe Side and More Hall Reservoir.*

SUMMARY
Much of this route passes through Forestry Commission land at Wharncliffe Woods. Bear in mind there is no legal right of way here and bridleways are not generally waymarked once you pass into the Commission's woods. Having said this the delightful woods you pass through at the beginning are waymarked initially. Virtually all the tracks in the woods are perfect for those of intermediate skill, being largely wide and fairly smooth surfaced.

The route is in a sense arbitrary, as there are numerous tracks suitable for bikes running through the woods, making it a veritable biker's playground, with numerous permutations. However this route com-

pletes the journey through the woods down the side of the Don Valley with a superbly effortless road section after the hard work in the forest. You can see a great distance over the plain to the north-east from the ridge that the road follows, making it a doubly pleasing return to your starting point. You will see why I chose the road to return instead of returning through the woods, if you go on a clear sunny day.

S Leave the village by heading north-west, past the Old Red Lion pub on the right. Immediately on your left pick up the ¶O that runs parallel to Woodhead Road. Shortly take the first ¶O L into the woods, away from the road. At the first ¶O T-junction go **R**. Follow the main track, past a minor crossroads after a field through trees on the left, going straight on as waymarked. Shortly you reach a very wide track.

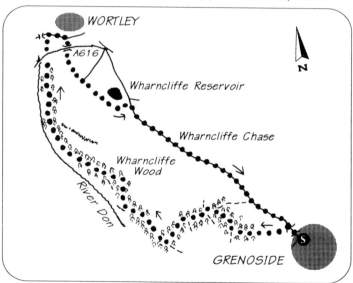

Go **L** downhill (as you can see right following **O** sign returns to the road). Through a gate part way down the track and at a split bear **R** following the main track at the bottom of the hill. Note a field brushes the track on the right and there is an information notice about access to Wharncliffe Chase on the right; this is the land immediately above the woods owned by a private estates company.

Go **R** at the next two splits which should bring you to a clear T-junction of rough tracks, with good views over the valley in front of you; you may be able to see the start of the Sheffield suburbs to your left, down the valley. Go **R** here and onto a slightly smaller track. Shortly on this track another field intrudes on the right and you can just see a radio mast at the back of it. The track drops steeply under power lines to a T-junction. **R** takes you back uphill, back under the power lines and climb fairly steeply, going **L** at the first split and **L** at the next T-junction.

Descend a rocky track to rejoin the main wide track and go **R** carrying on to descend under pylons again. At the next split ignore the smaller track left and stay on the main track **R**. Descend under pylons once more and ignore a minor left shortly before a track leads off behind you, through large square stone gateposts. Ignore this also, carrying on the main track, to go under the A616 and out of the woods, by a riding school on the left. Follow the track to a T-junction with the road.

Go **R** uphill and take the first minor **R ¶O** (*Ash Barn*). Follow the hard track **O** under the A616 again and at the T-junction go **R** for Gosling Moor Farm. Follow the track as it becomes rougher into trees, passing a farm a little distance to the left. Through a gate to the next gate where a tarmac road joins from the left. Ignore this and go straight through a gate towards farm buildings. Pass through, close to the buildings and along the track past the reservoir glimpsed through trees on the left.

As the main track goes round a left hand bend don't be distracted by the waymarked **O** through a small gate into a field straight ahead. Carry on round the bend to a T-junction with a road. **R** will take you along a spectacular ridge and back into Grenoside, your starting point.

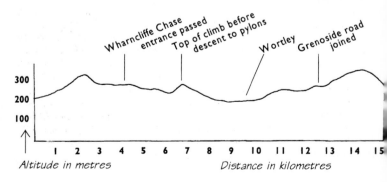

Altitude in metres

Distance in kilometres

14

LADYBOWER RESERVOIR

START *Ashopton Viaduct*   *Grid ref. 186866*

DISTANCE COVERED *15km/9¼ miles*
On road *8km/5miles*   **Off road** *7km/4¼ miles*

TIME ALLOWED *2½ hours*

GRADIENT DIFFICULTY *2 (with grade 3 climb - possible push/carry)*

ACCESS Car *Car park on westerly side of Ashopton Viaduct.*
Train *Hope station.*

ORDNANCE SURVEY MAPS
1:50,000 - Landranger 110, Sheffield & Huddersfield
1:25,000 - Outdoor Leisure Map 1, The Peak District - Dark Peak

SUGGESTED BREAK *The bridleway junction just after Lockerbrook
Farm. Stupendous views of the ridge of peaks south of Ladybower
Reservoir.*

SUMMARY
*Although strictly speaking this route is in Derbyshire it has been
included because of its proximity to Sheffield, the main city of South
Yorkshire, and also because of the spectacular scenery witnessed. Be
warned however this area of the Peak National Park becomes
phenomenally busy at weekends and every day throughout the
summer months. It's easy to see why when you've witnessed the
scenery.*

*The generally smooth gradients make this a good introduction to
those wanting to step up from beginner's level. There is only one
extremely challenging climb where you will probably have to dismount - see profile.*

S From the car park go back across the viaduct on the A57 ignoring the left for Derwent Valley just before it. Immediately over the viaduct go first **L** on an unmarked track. Stay on this main track, as shortly after twisting around a small inlet it turns into a road. Continue to follow the east bank of Ladybower Reservoir. Shortly after the telephone box at Old House the road takes a wide 180 degree swing to the left to give you a good view of the ornate towers of the imposing dark stone dam to the right.

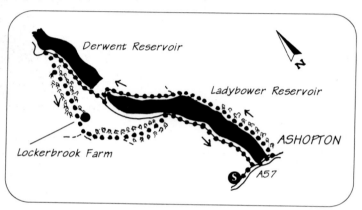

Follow the road to the roundabout in the woods. Go **R** here with another good view on the right of the dam past the commemorative plaque. Continue on the road until it bends left and downhill, by an inlet on the right. Just after the bend look out for a ¶O on the **L** (*Snake Road 2*). There is a very steep but relatively short climb through the woods until the path starts to climb more gradually and you can remount.

The track comes out of the woods but remains close to them on the left. Follow the rocky track downhill with no troublesome junctions on the way, past Lockerbrook Farm on the left to a ¶ junction of 4 **O**.

Take the **L** for Crookhill Farm leading up a small, steep bank to a wide grass track scarred by heavy vehicle tracks. At the end of the field take the O¶ **L** through trees to Derwent. Be warned: this track gets progressively steeper. At the T-junction with the road at the bottom bear **R**. Follow the west bank of the reservoir back to the T-junction with the main road and **R** to take you back to your parking spot.

Ladybower Reservoir

ALONG THE WAY

• <u>Spectacular views</u> greet you periodically through the trees going over Lockerbrook heights, as Derwent Edge can be seen to the east. The crowning glory of this run is the view at the bridleway crossroads just after Lockerbrook farm. The good views of the peaks to the south west continue along open Hagg, before your descent of Hagg Side.

• <u>The commemorative plaque</u> just after passing the side of the dam after the roundabout turning is incredibly poignant. I won't spoil the surprise by revealing the brief story it tells other than to say it concerns a dog. You must do the route yourself to discover what happened!

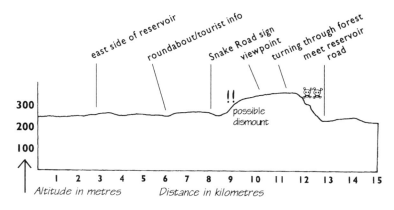

15

THURLSTONE & MIDHOPE MOORS

START *Penistone* *Grid ref. 218032*

DISTANCE COVERED *18km/11miles*
On road *6km/3¾ miles* **Off road** *12km/7¼ miles*

TIME ALLOWED *3 hours* **GRADIENT DIFFICULTY** *2/3*

ACCESS *Start from the town centre.* **Car** *There are plenty of small streets near the starting point at the junction of the A628 and B6106 in Millhouse Green.* **Train** *Penistone station.*

ORDNANCE SURVEY MAPS
1:50,000 - Landranger 110, Sheffield & Huddersfield
1:25,000 - Outdoor Leisure 1, Peak District, Dark Peak (1995edition)

SUGGESTED BREAK *The bridge at the head of Langsett Reservoir before the climb onto Midhope Moors.*

SUMMARY
This ride is more difficult than may appear at face value. Firstly it's at a relatively higher altitude than the other runs and will be a few degrees colder; quite often there are stronger winds on the moortops, even on some mild summer days. Secondly some of the bridleways are rather narrow and can become very muddy. It really all depends on the time of year, the recent weather and your own skill as a rider! The rest of the off road sections are generally fairly easily with a lovely wide descent down from Midhope Moors. The route takes you into the Peak National Park and there are numerous glorious views at many points along the way. A very beautiful run, especially on a warm, still summer's day!

S Leave the town centre on the A628 Manchester road and head into Millhouse Green. Shortly after entering here the route proper starts as the B6106 to Holmfirth splits off **R.** Take this road and turn **L**

onto the first ¶O. Follow this tarmac road to the buildings at the end, and bear left down the side of them to cross a small bridge over the river Don. The path may get a bit sticky up the next small hill leading through a gate and past a private house on the right. Follow the tarmac road to a T-junction and **R** which takes you straight into a farmyard. Look out for the small white arrow painted on the corner of a building which directs you through a yard to a gate.

Through the gate the route briefly turns into a landrover track and descends to a small beck feeding the stream on the right. At the first minor split branch off the main road onto a minor track to the **L** which takes you alongside a small ridge, site of a dismantled railway and shortly under a bridge (the old railway went across the top). Bear 90 degrees **R** as soon as you emerge from the bridge and follow this until you come to a T-junction with a well made farm track.

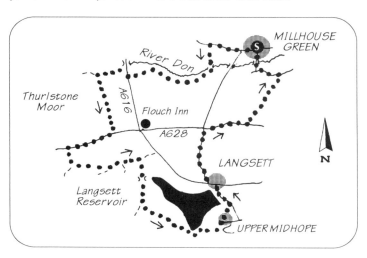

Bear **L** towards the farm house (Hazelhead) you can see, and pass in front of it keeping it on your right. Follow this well made road to the main A616 and go **R**. Very shortly take the ¶O on the **L**, just before the old railway bridge over the road ahead. Go past a couple of houses until a gate; a blue arrow directs you 90 degrees to the **L** through a smaller gate, as the track that goes straight on turns into a footpath and a sign prohibits cycling.

Follow this narrow track over Thurlstone Moor, emerging after nearly 2km onto the **EXTREMELY BUSY A628.** Go **R** here (riding on the verge is advisable!) then in just over 1km there is a **¶O** on the **L** just past Delmont Grange farmhouse. The **¶O** splits off **L** and the main farm track carries on to the right. You know you are on the right track as a **O** is waymarked at the next gate. The very wide, rough track meets a T-junction at the end where you go **L**. At the next split follow the waymarking **L** (footpath waymarked right).

The track leads through the woods to a very acute T-junction. Go **R** here looking out for the **¶** telling you you are on the way to the Derwent and Ashop Valleys. This good track leads out of the woods and ignoring a couple of waymarked footpaths to the left, drop down to a bridge - a good place for lunch on the banks by the small weir.

After crossing the bridge over the weir carry on through the small gate and straight on (don't follow what appears to be a small path leading to the right alongside the river). Climb steeply with woods on your left - it's rocky and steep and I was unable to do this without quite a few 'feet down' - a real 'expert' section. The terrain levels out coming onto the openness of Midhope Moors. This sporadically bumpy track leads to a waymarker about 2km after the stream. Follow the familiar blue arrow, doubling back **L** towards Langsett Reservoir.

The track that continues straight on is in fact still a bridleway, though not waymarked. You can explore this if you feel like lengthening the route, but you will have to double back on yourself and ultimately take the previous left to the reservoir; the track straight on reaches Derwent Reservoir after 5km.

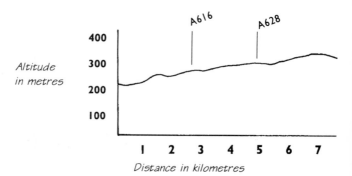

74

A nice long downhill run leads you through ruined buildings and back into woods at the side of the reservoir. Go over a small bridge over a feeder stream for the reservoir and continue on the track until meeting the road again, on a hairpin bend. Go **L** ¶ *Upper Midhope ¼ and Langsett ¾*. On the first right hand bend just coming into Upper Midhope take a small **L**, marked *no through road for motor vehicles* and *Manor Farm*.

Coming into Manor Farm take the ¶**O** to the **R**. Stay on this track till meeting the metalled road again and go **L**, taking you over the dam at the eastern end of Langsett Reservoir. On meeting the A616 by the Waggon and Horses pub go **L**. Take the first **R** up Gilbert Hill until you meet the main road. Turn 90 degrees **R** here onto a minor road ¶ *Hunshelf*. Climb on this hill until the first ¶**O** on the **L** which leads you to the left of a small summit.

A short, sticky and narrow uphill section eventually widens and begins to descend after being joined by a footpath from the right. After ¾km of descent join the very minor road in the hamlet of Hill Side and go **L**. After passing over a dismantled railway at the next T-junction go **R** onto Parkin House Lane. Dropping down into Millhouse Green you hit the A628 and go **L** ending up back at the starting point where the B6106 splits off right from this road.

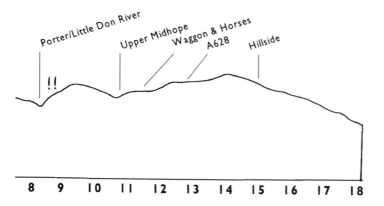

16

EMLEY MOOR

START *Horbury Bridge*   *Grid ref. 278178*

DISTANCE COVERED *22km/13½ miles*
On road *13km/8 miles*   **Off road** *9km/5½ miles*

TIME ALLOWED *3 hours*

GRADIENT DIFFICULTY *2 - but many ups and downs*

ACCESS *Start from the east of Horbury Bridge.* **Car** *Some parking on minor roads off the main A642 as it crosses the Calder & Hebble Navigation.* **Train** *Ravensthorpe station on the Huddersfield line (5km).*

ORDNANCE SURVEY MAPS
1:50,000 - Landranger 110, Sheffield & Huddersfield
1:25,000 - Pathfinder 703, Wakefield (South) & Area

SUMMARY
South of the urban mass that makes up much of the centre of West Yorkshire, the heavy concentration of buildings breaks up as the cityscape begins to disappear and small towns and villages dot the rolling hills that rise further west to become the Pennines.

This is ideal biking country for those wanting a taste of the challenge of mountain biking without the steeper more challenging gradients, say of the real 'Pennine' runs of Calderdale. Before getting onto Emley Moor the route is characterised by a series of relatively small ups and downs. The climb onto Emley Moor takes you to about 200m (650ft), but this moderate height is quite enough to give you good views over much of the south east of Kirklees. Be aware that after heavy rain and for much of the time outside the summer months the last part of the run into Coxley may be muddy because of use by horses.

S From the east end of Horbury Bridge go westwards on the A642 from Wakefield to Huddersfield. Passing under a disused railway viaduct, take the first **R** to climb up Hostingley Lane, passing Mitchell's camping shop at the bottom on the left. After 1km look out for a **¶O** on the **L** which drops quickly to take you over Smithy Brook. Follow the track up the field and straight over the next road, continuing on a **¶O**. At the T-junction with the road **R** takes you back over Smithy Brook and first **L** takes you along Thornhill Edge, on Edge Road.

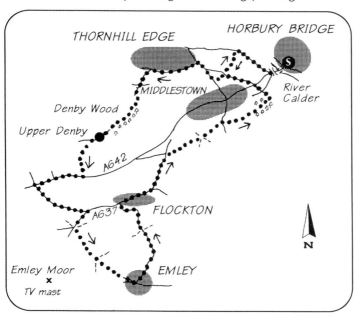

Passing through the settlement look for a **L** onto Judy Haigh Lane, just before a T-junction with Edge Junction/Albion Rd. Drop down and up over Howroyd Beck, and going **R** at the split and straight over. Follow onto an unsignposted **O** as the road bends to the right of iron gates in front of a house. Follow the track round the back of the house and climb, following Denby Wood on your left. Follow the main track climbing gradually through farm buildings. There are good valley views on the left with the woods on the other side. Come off the rough track and onto the tarmac road through Upper Denby.

Just departing the hamlet, and after the ¶ track on the right for a footpath and O, the road forks. Take the L onto a rough unsigned O off the road. Again climb gradually uphill to emerge out of a field gate into a small settlement. Continue on the tarmac road to the main road. At the T-junction with the A642 bear R and at the roundabout L ¶ Flockton. Just as you enter Flockton look for the first R going down and uphill to the next set of junctions known as Six Lanes End.

Ride onto the rough byway, second on the L (Crawshaw Lane). Follow the track to a three way split and take the middle option, leading into the rear of Emley (the left hand track is a footpath down a private road to Upper Crawshaw Farm). Join the tarmac road uphill to a T-junction and go L. Take the second L down Church Street, past the post office and church, following the road out of Emley village. Stay on this road for about 2km, coming to a T-junction with the main road in Flockton and going R. Pass through Flockton and take the first major L, just before the road starts to swing right, out of Flockton.

As you come to a small row of houses on the left look for an unmarked track, a O, on the R at the start of the houses (the houses themselves are just before Grange Lane on the left), passing through smallholdings, then into more open country. Follow this track to a rough crossroads and straight over (ignoring a gated track just to your right as you cross). Follow this track to emerge through houses onto a road. G R then immediate L down a ¶O.

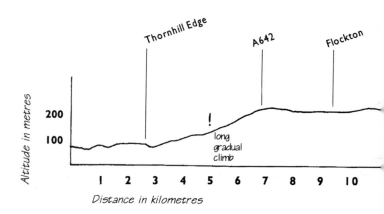

Descend into woods and past a pond down on your right. After a small climb and drop, go through houses to a T-junction and **L** to the main road. Cross straight over and straight over the next road, the A642. Shortly after a **¶O** on the left reach a **O** crossroads and go **R**. You are now on the track down to Smithy Brook, used to start your route. Go back on this track to Hostingley Lane.

ALONG THE WAY

• <u>_Emley Moor TV Mast_</u> _This huge structure is in your sights for much of the ascent onto the moor. At 1084 feet it is taller than the Eiffel Tower, making it the tallest unsupported structure in the UK._

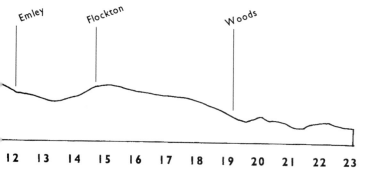

17

MELTHAM COP

START   Castle Hill, Huddersfield   Grid ref. 152141

DISTANCE COVERED 22½km/14 miles
On road   12km/7½ miles   **Off road**   10½km/6½ miles

TIME ALLOWED 3½ hours   **GRADIENT DIFFICULTY** Difficult 2

ACCESS Car Start from the car park on top of Castle Hill. **Train** Berry Brow and Honley stations on the Penistone line, south of Huddersfield are very near the start of the route.

ORDNANCE SURVEY MAPS
1:50,000 - Landranger 110, Sheffield & Huddersfield
1:25,000 - Pathfinder 702, Huddersfield & Marsden

SUGGESTED BREAK The quiet bridleway south of Meltham Cop gives you a chance to savour the landscape as it gradually climbs to Meltham Moor.

SUMMARY
Although much of this route is on roads the bridleways are generally good quality, and it would be a pity to let this fact alone put you off this area which boasts fine rolling scenery. The green hills dip and slant into the dykes and hills in this south western corner of Kirklees and the moderate altitude make this a pleasant and inviting run.

Perhaps the scenic highlight is the view towards Meltham Moor from Meltham Cop. Views aside, the most challenging gradients are on well made surfaces, so this ride is a good opportunity for those not comfortable on steep gradients combined with more difficult off road surfaces. Don't miss the opportunity to sample the delights of the Castle pub at the finish of the run; a superb starting point combining a refreshment opportunity with great views over Huddersfield.

S From the car park follow Hill Side down to the T-junction and **R** to another T-junction. Go **L** here and take the next rough track **R** (no ¶), just past 'Stedding' bungalow. At the first split bear **R** on the less well surfaced track. Pass through a small settlement with a renovated barn an obvious feature and continue on this track to the road. Go **L** here and descend to a T-junction with a more main road and **L** again.

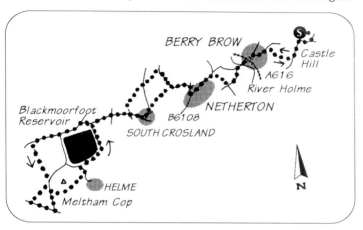

Under the railway bridge follow the main road downhill, past a post office on the left. Cross over the main road onto Stockwell Hill, dropping downhill and over the bridge. Take a first **L** shortly after the bridge onto Bank Foot Lane. Ascend steeply through trees on either side. As you emerge out of the woods and come to Hawkroyd Bank Road on the left, look for a small unsigned track directly opposite this road on your **R**. This leads you between the backs of houses on the left and woods on the right. Follow the main track past the end of the houses to a T-junction and go **R** downhill through woods.

At the next rough crossroads go **L** staying on the main track and ignoring one minor right. Follow it downhill to the B6108 opposite Butternab Road. Go **L** onto the B6108 and climb for about 1km. On the **R** look out for a very minor turning onto a narrow tarmac road by a small block of terraces on the right. Descend on this road under a railway bridge and uphill to a T-junction. Go **L** here onto a steep cobbled road. Bear **L** as you come to Delves Farm at the top of the hill (right by the farm is marked as private).

Follow the track straight on, ignoring the first left. Take the next **L** onto a track - you should pass over boulders at the start of the entrance, and under electricity wires. Follow it to a rough T-junction and **L**, still on the byway. Cross straight over the next road, staying on the rough track and to farm buildings. Go **L** here as the track becomes tarmac. Go **R** at a T-junction with a road to a crossroads and straight over, ¶ *Blackmoorfoot*. Stay on this road past Tom Cobleigh's pub on the right and ascending. Past the first left turn take the first **¶O L**, which brings you onto a wide **O**, actually on Black Moor.

Follow the **O** to the end, meeting a road opposite Wills o' Nats pub. At this junction go immediate **R** onto another **O**. At the end go **L** onto the Slaithwaite Road. Go first **L** again and **R** down the first **¶O**, following the foot of the large grassy hillock known as Meltham Cop on your left. At the end of the **O** go **L** on the road and shortly downhill **R** onto the rough track taking you past the southern side of Blackmoorfoot Reservoir on the left. Bend 90 degrees left when reaching the house at the end of this track onto a road. Follow it to the main road and go **R**.

Retrace your earlier steps over the crossroads onto Intake Lane. Carry straight on this road into the small settlement of South Crosland and take the first minor **L ¶** *Crosland Moor*. Take the first track on the **R** just

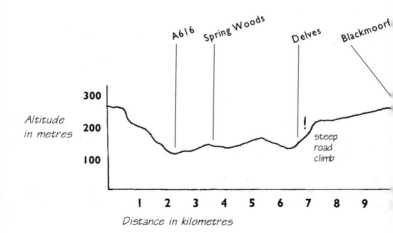

past Green Gate Knoll bungalow. Follow this track to the T-junction at the end and go **R**. Retrace your earlier steps past Delves Farm and **R** to take you under the railway bridge. Meet the main road and go **L** downhill. As you pass Butternab Road on the left, take a **R** down Armitage Road (¶ *Holme Valley Business Centre*). Follow it as it bends round right and passes the business centre on the right (mill buildings) and over the river.

Bear left up Carriage Drive to the main road and go **R**. Take the first **L** ¶ *Newsome ¾*. You can now follow your outward route, under the railway bridge and **R** up Lady House Lane. Pick up the byway up Cold Hill Lane, back up to the road. **L** leads you towards Castle Hill. Retrace your steps **R** and **L** up Hill Side.

ALONG THE WAY
•Castle Hill is literally built on history. Ancient British earthworks, occupied since 2000 BC, they have become a local beauty spot. Great views of your intended route and the Victorian Jubilee Tower make this an ideal starting point. The tower can be ascended.

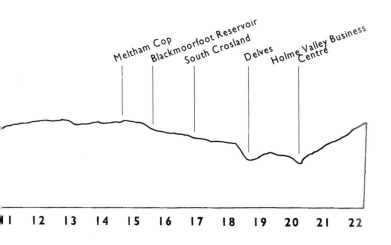

18

HOLME VALLEY

START *Meltham*   *Grid ref. 104102*

DISTANCE COVERED   *22km/13½miles*
On road *9km/5½ miles*   **Off road** *13km/8 miles*

TIME ALLOWED *3½ hours*   **GRADIENT DIFFICULTY** *2/3*

ACCESS Car *Entering Meltham on the B6107 from Holmfirth, look for the left onto a wide road (Royd Road) where there is ample parking.*
Train *Honley station on the Penistone line south of Huddersfield.*

ORDNANCE SURVEY MAPS
1:50,000 - Landranger 110, Sheffield & Huddersfield
*1:25,000 - Pathfinder 714, Holmfirth & Saddleworth Moor **or***
        Outdoor Leisure 1, Peak District, Dark Peak (1995 edition)

SUGGESTED BREAK *Ample quiet stopping points around the head of the Holme Valley, by Yateholme and Riding Wood reservoirs.*

SUMMARY
Although this is a fairly hard and long route the tracks are ideal for mountain biking; wide and well made and none of the climbs are ridiculously steep. The views from the long track descending to Digley Reservoir are quite superb as are many of the views below Holme Moss TV mast, at the head of the Holme Valley. Although climbs are similarly steep to the Castle Hill route the immediate scenery is definitely one of Pennine grandeur, so be sure to go well prepared for any unpredictable weather on the tops.

S   Ascend Royd Road ignoring the first **¶O** on the left. Take the second **¶O L**, off the tarmac road leading to Ash Royd Farm, onto the track. A good hard climb levels out, with good views to your left towards Castle Hill. Drop down into the beautiful woods at the top of Harden Clough and shortly to the main road. Turn **R** onto the main road and in about 1km **L** down a **¶O**. Enjoy the great view of Marsden Clough as you descend. The **O** doubles back 180 degrees as a footpath to Wessenden Head Moor carries straight on.

Follow the main track ignoring any minor turnings bringing you through a gate to a road, above Digley Reservoir down to your right. Go **R** at this T-junction and then **R** at the next crossroads, **¶** *Holme*. Take the next **R** after the steep descent which takes you onto the top of the dam wall with the reservoir on the right. This road leads to a T-junction with the road by the Holme Castle country hotel and go **R**.

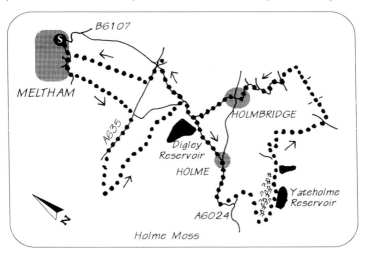

Exit Holme on this road and wend your way on the main road, with the Holme Moss TV mast ever present ahead of you. After about 1km on the main road, after a small bridge at the head of Rake's Dike, look for an unsignposted track **L**. Simply follow the main track on a very enjoyable ride through conifers and past the steep grassy banks of Yateholme Reservoir on the right. Eventually cross over the dam wall of Riding Wood Reservoir which is on your right.

The road bends left, and opposite the house just after the bend take the **¶O R**. Ascend through the conifers and follow the main track round a large right hand hairpin. Ascending still, at the next junction, bear **L** away from the track that goes straight on below Ramsden Edge.

Climb on this track continuing to the junction with the road. Go straight across the tarmac road onto another track. Keep straight on over a minor crossroads and straight onto the tarmac road. Take the unsignposted track **L** just before new looking grey metal sheds.

Continue on the track passing a quarry entrance on the left, to the road and straight over onto another track, again to a road. Go **R** at this junction to descend steeply into Dobb. Just past the primary school on the right turn immediate **L** onto Dobb Top Lane. Continue going **R** at every opportunity until meeting the main road. Go **R** here, over the river and past the church. **L** in front of the Bridge Tavern takes you up Field End Lane. Take a **L** onto Bank Top Lane with beautiful woods on the left.

Stay on this road past Digley Reservoir on the left, bending and climbing to go straight over a crossroads. Continue on this road (Green Gate Road) to the crossroads at the Ford Inn and **L** onto the main road. By the sign for the Huntsman Inn on the right take a **¶O R**. Follow the track straight on past Harden Hill Farm on the right onto the grass track. An exciting, steepish descent leads back to the T-junction with Royd Road. **R** will lead you back to Meltham.

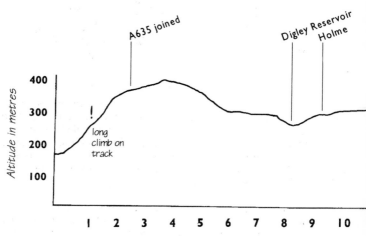

The Holme Valley from Holme Moss

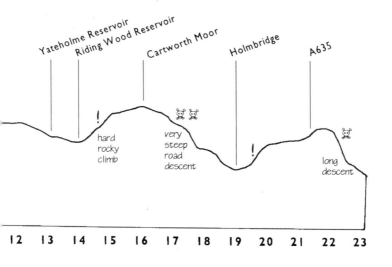

Yateholme Reservoir
Riding Wood Reservoir
Cartworth Moor
Holmbridge
A635

hard
rocky
climb

very
steep
road
descent

long
descent

12 13 14 15 16 17 18 19 20 21 22 23

19

ABOVE RIPPONDEN

START *Ripponden*   *Grid ref. 040198*

DISTANCE COVERED *13km/8 miles*
On road *6km/3¾ miles*   **Off road** *7km/4¼ miles*

TIME ALLOWED *2 hours*

GRADIENT DIFFICULTY *2 (optional climb from Ripponden is 3)*

ACCESS *Start from Ripponden centre. **Car** Car park on Royd Lane coming into Ripponden, just before the main road splits in the centre. For the route without the steep climb there is a rough parking area opposite the pub at the top of this hill. **Train** Sowerby Bridge is 5km from Ripponden on the very busy A58 road. A longer route on the south of the valley along Butterworth End Lane involves steep climbs.*

ORDNANCE SURVEY MAPS
1:50,000 - Landranger 104, Leeds, Bradford & Harrogate
              Landranger 110, Sheffield & Huddersfield (small section)
1:25,000 - Outdoor Leisure 21, South Pennines

SUGGESTED BREAK *If you can find a sheltered spot on the Calderdale Way/Water Stalls Road section there are great views over the moors to your left and down much of Calderdale.*

SUMMARY
This route gives you a taste of West Yorkshire's bleak and beautiful moorland scenery. If you start above the Ryburn Valley by the pub car park you miss a spectacular final descent, but avoid a very steep initial climb. After the steep climb out of Ripponden the topography is relatively flat with off road riding mainly on wide tracks used by farm vehicles. The descent after Long Edge Moor road takes you down narrow and tricky paths where skill is needed.

This is rewarded when arriving at the picturesque settlement of *Cotton Stones* before a final road section and the optional steep descent down to the valley. The tracks around *Long Edge Moor* section are widely used by horses so take care and slow down when passing them. I've only completed the route in spring months but I imagine some of the tracks will get very sticky in winter.

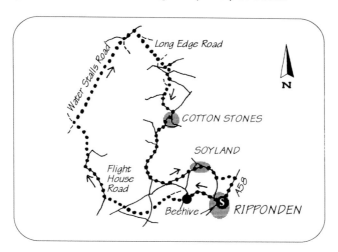

If starting in Ripponden take a **R** up Royd Lane, approaching on the A58 from Sowerby Bridge (just before the main road splits). Climb this very long, steep hill. At the top emerge on the road by the Beehive pub. **This is a good alternative starting point if you wish to avoid a very steep climb and descent. Parking opposite Beehive pub.**

Head down the **O¶** *Cote Road* on the opposite side of the road. At a junction with the **O** of Cote Road by a farm, go **L**. Follow this track to a split and go **L** to a road. Slightly to the left is a **O¶** *London Spring Road*. Follow the track past a farmhouse, joining a firmer track here and carrying straight onto it, to a T-junction with a road at the end. Go straight across this road to a **¶** for two **O**. Take the **L** one **¶** *Flight House Road* (ignore the one to Merry Bent). **R** onto the road at the end of this **O**, past moorland on the left. Look for the first **O L ¶** *Greaves Head Road*, after about 1km on this road. Follow it past disused quarries. At the first fork bear **L**, as the right goes to Flint Hall.

Ignore the next main track to the right and continue straight to a **O** crossroads with the Calderdale Way. To the left is a Yorkshire Water permissive footpath. Go **R ¶** *Calderdale Way.* Follow this track until the Calderdale Way is waymarked to the left, just after a gate. Carry straight on (passing a waymarked footpath on the right) on a green track, shortly going through a gate past a quarry on the right. Continue past farm buildings to a tarmac road and bear **L** onto it, taking you to the main road at the end (noting the **O** you have exited on is **¶** *Water Stalls Road*).

Ignoring the right **¶** as private to Crow Hill Farm, go **R** onto the main road. Take the next **O** off this road on the **R**, **¶** *Long Edge Road.* Go **R** at the first split (ignoring left **¶** *Wine Tavern Road*). Carry on to a rough T-junction, going straight on to the road. **L** takes you past the road name Red Brink Lane and shortly after this down a steep **O** to the **R**. Cross straight over the next road to a T-junction and go **L**. Descend to the first buildings (boarding kennels) and **R** down the first **¶O** track, opposite these buildings. Descend and bear left in front of a farm gate, down a very narrow, rocky section to the road.

Join the road and go **L** to a T-junction at the back of Cotton Stones. Go **R** at this T-junction and **R** at the back of the church. Continue over a bridge and ascend past the Alma Inn on the left. Remain on this road for about 1½km, dipping down over a bridge and climbing to a split

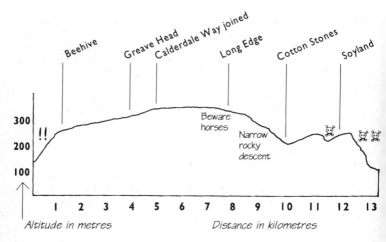

in the road bearing **L**. At the next staggered crossroads where Blue Ball Road joins from the right go **L**, and into the settlement of Soyland **(Just coming into this settlement on Lane Head Road a R takes you back to the 'easy' starting point next to the Beehive Inn).**

If descending back into Ripponden carry on through this settlement on this road. Ignore any minor turnings and pass through the next settlement of Soyland Town, until you see a **¶O** on the **L** just past a bench. Descend until the grassy track jinks 90 degrees right and turn **L** just after this (not **¶**). Descend through houses on Ryburn Lane to the A58 and **R** back to Ripponden.

ALONG THE WAY
• <u>The Stoodley Pike Monument</u> *This can clearly be seen at the far side of Turley Holes and Higher House Moor on the Calderdale Way/ Water Stalls Road section. Originally built by local subscription to celebrate victory over Napoleon in 1814, the present monument was completed in 1856 after being struck by lightning. It has a public viewing gallery 40ft up its 120ft height. Its purpose is radically different to traditional post world war one and two monuments which usually mourn the loss of the dead or the 'glory' of victory; an inscription on it makes clear it celebrates the outbreak of peace.*

Descent towards Ripponden

LUDDENDEN DEAN

START *Luddenden Foot*   *Grid ref. 037250*

DISTANCE COVERED *15km/9½ miles*
On road *7km/4½ miles*   **Off road** *8km/5 miles*

TIME ALLOWED *3 hours*   **GRADIENT DIFFICULTY** *3*

ACCESS Car *Coming into Luddenden Foot on the A646 from Sowerby Bridge turn **L** just after the post office. There is a car park just after the canal bridge and also plenty of parking as the road widens and goes over the river.* **Train** *From Mytholmroyd station. You may cycle back to Luddenden Foot using the quieter Scout Road/Sowerby Lane on the south of the valley. This brings you into Luddenden Foot over the railway and onto the A646. Though it adds a few kilometres it avoids the heavy traffic of the very busy A646.*

ORDNANCE SURVEY MAPS
1:50,000 - Landranger 104 - Leeds, Bradford & Harrogate
1:25,000 - Outdoor Leisure 21, South Pennines

SUGGESTED BREAK *You should be able to pick a good quiet spot along the road leading through Upper Throstle and Upper Saltonstall.*

SUMMARY
The small network of valleys that feed the river Calder as it leads east towards Halifax have formed quite irregular shapes and gradients, making for both interesting scenery and very challenging and popular mountain biking. This is particularly evident on this route which takes you through the secluded villages of Luddenden and Booth before ascending onto the side of Midgley and Warley Moors.

Generally the first half of the route has some very steep climbs in places and whilst, in the main, descending after Wainstalls, some of these are hair-raising descents. The bridleways are almost without exception wide and of good quality; either hardpacked or cobbles (a real boneshaker). I take my hat off to anyone who can complete the climb up to High House Lane without stopping several times; don't worry if you have to walk it; it's physically and technically difficult.

S Go back to the **VERY BUSY** main A646 and **L** then first **R ¶** for Luddenden (Luddenden Lane) just past the Weavers Arms pub. Follow the road past a modern housing estate on the left and follow the **¶** into the village of Luddenden. Bearing **L** in Luddenden brings you to the front of the church by the Lord Nelson pub. A **¶O** leads you down the **L** side of the church, keeping a small brook on your right with the cemetery on the other side of it.

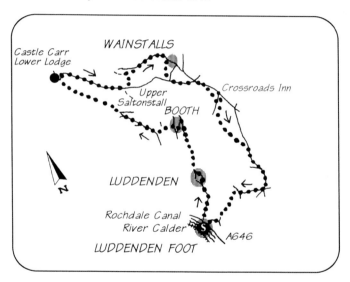

Keep following the obvious line of the track straight past a small row of terraces. Soon ascend a very small cobbled rise and double back almost 180 degrees on a cobbled road (no **¶**). A small water trough collecting spring water on the right is passed, and you begin to ascend steeply. Emerging at a T-junction with a tarmac road, go **R** and shortly take the first **¶O** on the **L** at the entrance to Booth Cricket Club. A steep climb takes you towards a farmyard and a blue waymarker on the wall directs you round a right bend as the gradient increases still further.

A further waymarker at the next mini T-junction takes you **L** to a T-junction with the tarmac road of High House Lane. Go **R** at the first turning, down Dry Carr Lane that is waymarked with the sign for the West Yorkshire Cycle Way (green wheel on white background). Ignore the next dead end track on the left and at the hairpin bend go straight on, ignoring the Cycle Way waymark that takes you round the hairpin. This track takes you through woods; follow it more or less in a straight line until you meet the fascinating Castle Carr Lower Lodge, and go under the middle of this castle-like lodge and bend right over the river. The track turns into a metalled road and follows the other side of the valley. Pass through the small settlement of Throstle Bower and into Upper Saltonstall.

After the lovely Throstle Bower, just as you enter Upper Saltonstall pass a marked footpath on the right and up a small rise take the first unmarked rough track on the **L** off the main road. The track goes past a house on the left and after several sharp turns go **R** onto the track marked Calderdale Way. At the T-junction with the tarmac road go **R** into Wainstalls. Shortly after coming into the start of the village look for a **¶O R** and follow it to rejoin the main road.

At the T-junction just after emerging onto this road go **L** towards the crossroads next to the Crossroads Inn. Go **R** here then very shortly look for an unsignposted **R** onto a **O** at Sandy Fore Farm next to a bus stop. Follow this main track to the road at the end and go **L**. Coming to the T-junction at the end of this road look for the **¶O** just before the actual junction on the **R**, (still on Stocks Lane). Follow this well made way through farms as it stays fairly level and **R** onto the tarmac road at the end.

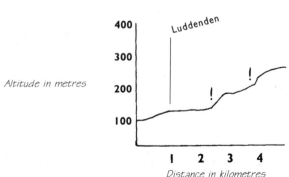

Altitude in metres

Distance in kilometres

Try and pick out Mytholmroyd and Stoodley Pike monument from the viewpoint at the end of this track. Descend quite steeply on this road to the intersection of five roads (in fact the second crossroads junction) and descend down Abbey Lane, the furthest to your **R** (unsuitable for large vehicles).

Shortly after Deep Lane joins from the left the road forks. Bear **L** here (road sign prohibits you if you are more than 7ft wide) and straight through the picturesque, whitewashed cottages just after Shepherd House. You are riding above the council estate at Luddenden Foot in the valley to your right, where you began the route. The track becomes steepish and **very bumpy; keep well under control on the brakes from here on down.** Take a **R** on meeting the road and **steep downhill** into the back of Luddenden Foot and to the main road. Go **R** onto the main road and **L** over the canal bridge to your car or the train station.

ALONG THE WAY

• <u>Castle Carr Lower Lodge</u> At the end of Luddenden Dean before rising to Throstle Bower, this highly stylised estate lodge was built by a textile baron in the last century and guarded a large private estate. After his and his son's death the majority of the grand estate fell into disrepair and this is one of the few surviving remnants.

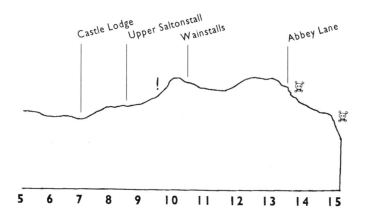

LOG OF THE RIDES

RIDE	DATE	NOTES
1		
2		
3		
4		
5		
6		
7		
8		
9		
10		
11		
12		
13		
14		
15		
16		
17		
18		
19		
20		